Simplify Government!

A fresh analysis of how the United States should be organized and run in the 21rst Century.

By Fred Krueger.

Fred Krueger
3100 Donald Douglas Loop North, #7
Santa Monica, CA 90405

Simplify Government!/ Fred Krueger. —1st edition.

ISBN 978-1500428136

Dedicated to my friend and fellow investor Jim Willenborg many of whose simple, straightforward ideas rang true to me.

"Simplicity is not the absence of clutter, that's a consequence of simplicity. Simplicity is somehow essentially describing the purpose and place of an object and product. The absence of clutter is just a clutter-free product. That's not simple."

Joni Ive, head designer Apple

"I think I've been in the top 5% of my age cohort all my life in understanding the power of incentives, and all my life I've underestimated it. Never a year passes that I don't get some surprise that pushes my limit a little farther"

Charlie Munger, Berkshire Hathaway

"Simple – Yes. Easy – No."

Yoda, Star Wars

Table of Contents

I. Introduction

OUR COUNTRY STARTED OUT WITH A SIMPLE DOCUMENT. The Constitution of the United States, written in 1787, is a mere 4,435 words long – about 20 pages. Those 20 pages were enough to define the world's first modern democracy: separation of powers between the President, the Congress, the Senate, and the Judicial system; and a procedure for adding amendments. Over the next 200 years, 27 of these were added – most of them a single sentence in length.

But while the legal backbone of our country is still very succinct, the reality of our political, judicial and economic system is anything but. Our tax code is now 73,954 pages long[1]. At twenty pages per day, it would require 10 years of nonstop reading for an individual to parse it in its entirety. Obama's health care bill was 1,018 pages, Clinton's 1,342. It's safe to assume that the majority of our lawmakers only have a summary understanding of the very laws they are promoting.

In 2010, the US Defense budget was $533 Billion Dollars. An additional $160 Billion was spent on "overseas contingency operations" for the "war on terror", another $70 Billion for Homeland Security, $53 Billion for the NSA and $108 Billion by The Office of Veteran Affairs. All told, $923 Billion Dollars was spent on defense in 2010 – while all individual income taxes totaled just $898 Billion dollars. In other words, 103% of all individual income taxes went to the military – and this at a time when the US *was not at war.* The fact that the budgetary process is so complex has allowed an absurdity like this to go virtually unnoticed.

Social Security was started by FDR in 1935, as a simple program to provide retirement benefits for lower income workers. Today it is an accounting and financial nightmare – on one hand making the budget look far better than it should (by including social security receipts in the plus column) – and on the other hand, taking into account the future liabilities of an increasingly aging population – being itself a problem of huge proportions.

Our medical system has evolved into an equally complex and dysfunctional monster. The average insurance plan is completely opaque – with some parts covered by the government, some parts not, and generally a form of Russian roulette on the part of the patient. Lose your job and get seriously ill – nobody will cover you; choose the wrong healthcare plan and you might get stuck with a bill that will bankrupt you. Despite spending 5.1% of the entire US GDP on health benefits (triple the percentage as under Carter), the state of the union on healthcare has never been worse.

The picture I am painting is of a system that has evolved into an unwieldy, out-of-control mess of complexity. What started out so simply, is, finally, after 200 years, a nightmare of exceptions, compromises, accounting double standards and off-balance sheet items. Both political parties are equally responsible – adding complexity on top of complexity to grab fine slices of special interest votes and political dollars.

This Kafka-esque situation is especially disturbing considering that in 2009 the United States came very close to a financial meltdown. The banking system, with the implicit guarantee of the US Government, was brought to its knees by activities in subprime mortgage collateralized bond obligations, a new, highly complex financial product that didn't even exist 10 years earlier. The solution to this problem: a 451 Page TARP bill, that lawmakers supposedly had a weekend to read and approve!

The purpose of this book is to address this situation head-on and argue that our fundamental problem is that the government has become too complex. We need to dramatically simplify it, starting from simple principals we should all be able to agree on. Government needs to be re-thought and re-invented in the same way that Google re-invented search and Apple re-invented the smart phone. We need a better, cleaner, smarter user interface for our country.

This is no simple task. Neither was the formation of the US government in the first place. In both cases, the key was to start with the correct idea. In 1776, that idea was a simple representative, democratic government, bound by the Constitution of the United States. In 2014, we need a similar radical re-think of where we are going, and use that idea to move towards execution. Form follows function.

The Emergence of Simplicity as A Goal.

One of the great lessons of technology in the 21rst century has been that simplicity itself is the ultimate design goal for any advanced system. Up until about the year 1999 it was generally believed that *more* was always better: you wanted more knobs and dials on your stereo system, blender, and dishwasher, more   features in your word processor, more places to click on your Internet "portal".

It took 200 years of technological innovation for human be-ings to realize that machines shouldn't be complex – they should be simple. People laughed at Charlie Chaplin getting caught in the gears of a factory (*Modern Times, 1936*), but they still admired all those moving parts. From Jules Verne to the Cockpit of a 747, to the first ENNIAC computer, the fact that humans could build these amazingly complex machines was viewed as a great accomplishment.

Visionaries like Stanley Kubrick and Gene Rodenberry start-ed imaging a slicker, simpler future back in the late 1960s – but this vision was not universally shared. Steve Jobs pio-neered the idea of simple clean design in computers, but as of 1997 it appeared that he had lost the war to Microsoft – and its bloated Microsoft Office / Windows "Suites".

And then we turned the corner.

In 1999, Google launched a bare bones search product that did away with all the prior clutter of Yahoo, Excite, or Lycos – the three giant "Internet Portals". With no forums, movie listings, chat rooms, financial discussion areas, horoscopes or games this ultra-utilitarian service seemed like more of a toy than a serious offering.

But it was a very useful toy. It got people to the content they were looking for simply, quickly, and with no banner ads. It was almost like they had reduced the Internet to a single text entry box with a button labeled "Search". Like the HAL computer in "2001 A Space Odyssey", the power was what the service could do – and the user interface was as simple as possible.

Five years later, in 2005, a new service called Facebook emerged with, again, a very plain-vanilla social product. Like Google, it was not the first in its field. An earlier mainstream success, MySpace, that not only offered to "connect you" but also tried to introduce you to new music, offered you ways of adding glitter to your "MySpace page", and even showcased "viral MySpace videos" as part of their core offering. Facebook initially did far less, but with a much more simple, consistent UI.

In 2007, Apple released the first iPhone – another radical experiment in simplification. In a market that belonged to Nokia, Motorola and a few other players, Steve Jobs dared dream up a simplified smart phone – one without a keyboard, with a clean, minimal OS and small little apps that you could buy for a dollar each in the "app store". Steve Ballmer at Microsoft made fun of it. Seven years later, Apple has a market cap of 500 Billion dollars, more than any other company in the world.

Also in 2007, a small startup called Dropbox funded with a hundred thousand dollars created an ultra-simple cloud storage system. Drag your files to a "Dropbox" folder on your laptop and they automatically sync (and are backed up) to the cloud. Today, Dropbox has 175 million users and is widely used in all kinds of business applications. Like all the previous examples, it wasn't the first product in its category, it was just the simplest.

In 2008, Spotify launched a revolutionary music service based on the simple idea that you should be able to listen to any song, anywhere, for free. Pick songs, organize them in playlists, stream them from your phone or your computer. Amazingly simple idea, and completely compelling.

In 2010, Uber launched its first mobile app allowing anybody in San Francisco to get a town car in minutes. The app consists of a map showing the location of the cars and a button to order one, now. Once your order is in progress, you can track the arrival of your ride on your mobile device. Cab companies – with their antiquated dispatch systems – cannot compete. It is only a matter of time before Uber and its competitors put them all out of business.

In 2011, Nest Labs produced a simple, well designed thermostat that you can control via the Internet, and that learns from your living habits. The company was sold to Google 4 years later for 3 Billion dollars.

In 2013, Amazon expanded its e-commerce platform to groceries with Amazon Fresh[2], a simple online website. There is nothing high tech about the look and feel of Amazon Fresh – the magic is just that it works, and your groceries actually get delivered to you before dawn on your doorstep.

Also in 2013, a startup called Tinder, funded by Interactive Corp (IAC), created a new kind of dating app that dispensed of long profiles and just used a "yes / no" swiping system to match people in the same geography. One year later, there are 10 Million daily Tinder users.

The point of these canonical examples (and there are much more), is that since the beginning of this new century, simplicity has systematically won over complexity. Give people a simple, easy to use way to tap into technology and they will embrace it completely; the results will vastly exceed any preconceived expectations.

Smart companies in the Silicon Valley from Apple to Amazon to thousands of startups are using this new knowledge as a key weapon. As Joni Ive, the head designer for Apple noted – this goes far beyond "removing clutter". It's about finding the absolute essence of a product; the absence of clutter is merely a consequence.

The purpose of this book is to apply the same rigorous design methodology to the idea of government. If our country itself was a product, what would it look like? All things equal would you create another version of Microsoft Word with six toolbars, or would you create the next iPhone? If government was *designed* as opposed to just being improvised post-election, what would it be?

Simple Means Less

To simplify means to cut, back, to reduce. What if instead of over a hundred different programs to help the poor there was one – a simple taxable cash payment for people who people under the US poverty guidelines? What if instead of instead of fifty separate state medical assistance programs there was a simple, universal minimal coverage – payable in the form of a voucher that could be used by any participating doctor, as full or partial payment? What if there was no department of agriculture – to pay farmers to grow or not grow crops, or a department of energy to "advance energy technology and promote related innovation" as it professes to do?

The government is large and complex for many historical and systematic reasons– but *not* because it works better. The innovation that you see when you walk into an Apple Store – walking assistants with full mobile support, genius bar, electronic receipts – is conspicuously missing from your state DMV, or from your federal building in Washington DC. Instead, our government is a sea of paper, rules, auditors, lobbyists, legal exceptions barely belongs to the 20th century, let alone the 21st.

The Importance of Incentives

Not only do we understand the importance of simplicity in technology today, we also understand incentives and gamification far better than ever. As Charlie Munger famously said, "all my life I have underestimated the power of incentives".

Certainly, anybody who has ever employed a sales force knows that it all boils down to the sales commission plan. Build an achievable commission structure and sales people will hit their goals. Incentive businesses to relocate into your country or state and they will eventually move. Take a look at the entire country of Ireland, or the Research Triangle Park in North Carolina. The idea that either one would be a tech hub back in 1980 would have been laughable.

The work of Kahnman and Tversky has illuminated *why* people do the things they do. Give people a clear incentive, and their behavior will change. Even small incentives matter. Give people a little virtual badge if they are the first to "check in" to a new restaurant on Foursquare and they will display that badge with pride. Reward people with stars and points in games and online fitness programs and they ascend to higher and higher levels.

We now have half a century of data on how incentives work in the welfare state. Anybody still advocating Socialism can take a good look at Francois Holland's France to get some hard data on what happens when you do. Without an incentive to start companies, people *don't* start companies; without an incentive to work people *don't* work; without an incentive to not abuse the medical system people *will abuse* it to the maximum extent they can.

On the flip side, anybody wondering if low capital gains taxes are good for business need look no further than Ireland or Singapore. Low, and more importantly, *predictably low*, corporate taxes create prosperity – full stop. Again, the realization here is that its not just about being "pro business" it's about having simple rules and clear incentives to follow them.

After simplicity, the use of incentives should be the major design direction for how to build the next United States of America. Do we need more engineers? We should incentivize people to get engineering skills. Do we want more healthy people that require less medical assistance? Incentivize people to get healthy and fit. Do we want a cleaner environment? Incentivize solar energy and energy conservation.

Direct, easy-to-understand incentives work best. Pay people cash, as opposed to some obscure form of tax rebate. Give people badges that show them and others they have clearly hit the desired goal. If it works for video games, sales contests, fitness programs and elementary schools it will work for the nation at large.

Giving people a safety net is not an excuse for creating dependency on a bloated, inefficient welfare state. There needs to be clean, incremental upgrade path from state sponsored welfare, medical benefits and retirement assistance. People need to be incentivized at every single level to depend less on society as a whole.

This book.

With all this in mind, this book is an attempt to take a completely fresh look at the largest and most successful organization on the planet: the US government.

I am not a politician or an economist. I am a technologist and a businessman who calls the shots as I see them. I was raised in France by two American parents, and have spent half of my life in both economies; I have experienced socialism first hand, spent time in Japan watching that model disintegrate, and am extremely familiar with the inner workings and machinations of Wall Street. But most of my career I have involved in technology and startups, and what I see with the US is a bloated organization with bad software.

I realize that politicians on both sides of the aisle will view this book as "utopian" or, dare I say it, "simplistic", but I think that above all, at this stage we need a clear idea of where we need to go, as opposed to just a way to win the next election.

My political agenda is neither Republican nor Democrat. The ideas presented here will likely infuriate both parties; the book will make the case against large defense budgets, but also against our current welfare state, it will blame Bush for passing a reckless prescription coverage bill, but also Obama for adding complexity on top of complexity to produce a healthcare "solution" which is really the worst of all worlds.

I am also deliberately avoiding any religious or "lifestyle" issues. I don't believe that debating contraception, stem cells, gay marriage, abortion and gun control should be mixed with debating government deficits, healthcare and aid to the poor. The tea party did itself a huge disfavor by combining these agendas. My platform is fiscally responsible full stop, not "fiscally responsible and socially liberal." I'll point out that the lobbying influence of the NRA is disturbing, but frankly I am neither for nor against guns. Its an issue the courts should decide; we have much more important fish to fry.

If we are going to cut through the clutter our country finds itself in we need something dramatic and absolute, not just a few more laws added to the mix. Its not about creating a system that is "fair" it's about creating a better system, period.

While my ultimate focus is the United States, I have found it extremely valuable to compare our data and our problems with those of other countries. Most of the ideas presented here have been tried by some country at some time in history. Without trying to leave anybody out, I have focused much of my research on the UK, Germany and France in Western

Europe, China, Japan and Singapore in Asia, and Sweden as a unique Nordic model. Focusing primarily on those countries helps focus the discussion and frame our problems in a bigger context.

Wherever possible, I have tried to normalize every statistic by diving by Gross Domestic Product. GDP is not a perfect metric, but it's the only one that allows apple to apples comparisons across time and countries. Numbers in billions and trillions are easily forgotten and change faster than you can would otherwise think. I still remember, for example, when the US Budget deficit hit 100 Billion in 1982. 27 years later it hit 14 times that – at the mind boggling 1.4 Trillion dollar level. Normalizing by GDP is the only way one can keep these figures straight and have an intelligent conversation about economics.

Collecting statistics in 2014 with the Internet is orders of magnitudes easier than it was in 1977 when I started college. All kinds of data has been compiled by organizations such as the Heritage Foundation, the World Bank and the OECD. One of my goals was to aggregate this information together to present the reader with a clear, unbiased view of where we are.

The US Government, with its three million workers, its arcane accounting systems, antiquated voting machines, enormous tax code and massive debt is like an obsolete IBM Mainframe that we need to take out to the junk heap and replace with a new iPad. It won't be easy, but we did it once before, when we built this government in the first place back in 1776. We started simple, we need to get back to simple.

Bright Lines. Simple Formulas

A book with the title of "Simplify Government" should offer clear, bright-lined recommendations. We do.

- Every individual should have a separate login with the US Government. This is where you should vote, pay your taxes, collect your benefits and learn exactly where your tax dollars are going.

- Taxes should be a flat 20% on income earned. There should be no corporate tax, no alternative minimum taxes, no separate social security tax. Welfare payments should be taxable supplements for low income earners.

- There should be a balanced budget amendment. At the beginning of every year, a budget should be developed for the next 4 years in which each year is budgeted to have zero deficit.

- Defense spending should be set at a maximum of 5% of aggregate taxable income. Any deviation of this should require a super-majority vote in congress.

- Total Welfare Payments and Medical Assistance should be budgeted at most 5% of aggregate taxable income. Both should be taxable. Included in this budget should be incentives to increase the overall health of the US population, and incentives for education. It is cheaper to keep people fit than to cure them; and cheaper to educate people rather than keep them on welfare.

- If you are on welfare, there should be an economic incentive to add to your welfare payments by part-time or full-time work. There should be no instance where you "can't afford to leave welfare"

- There should be a national healthcare program, as opposed to the current state sponsored system. This program should only cover the basics, not optional or advanced treatment. Like welfare, the program should be upgrade-able at the patients choice. And even at the most basic level, patients should be able to choose their own doctors, and benefit from making more cost-effective choices.

- Social security payments should be budgeted at most 5% of total income earned, and should be taxable.

- The entire rest of the government, transportation, judicial, agriculture, etc. should be kept at an absolute top 5% of total receipts.

2. Why Thing Aren't Simple

Parkinson's Law

IN PHYSICS, THE SECOND LAW OF THERMODY-
NAMICS states that the entropy of any physical system can
only increase. We go from organized to disorganized, from
simple to complex, from useful work to wasted, chaotic energy. This is a fundamental fact of the universe in which we live
in and is often used to explain why we can't go back in time.

Left on their own, human defined systems, such as large corporations, political organizations and large product teams
tend to follow the second law. They get bigger, more complex, more bloated and more inefficient – *entirely on their own.*

In 1955, the British Naval Historian Cyril NorthCoat Parkinson noticed this phenomenon in the continued growth of the
British Admiralty, long after the sun had set on the British
empire. He noted in particular, that from 1914 to 1928, the
number of ships in the Navy dropped by 66% -- but the
number of Admirals doubled. Eventually, Parkinson conclud-
ed, the navy would have "more admirals than ships".

His findings, which he codified as "Parkinson's Law" is usually stated by saying that work expands to fill the available time.

ADMIRALTY STATISTICS			
	1914	1928	*Percentage Increase or Decrease*
Capital ships in commission..	62	20	− 67·74
Officers and men in Royal Navy	146,000	100,000	− 31·56
Dockyard workers.........	57,000	62,439	+ 9·54
Dockyard officials and clerks	3,249	4,558	− 40·28
Admiralty officials.........	2,000	3,569	+ 78·45

From 1914 to 1928 the number of ships in the Royal Navy went down by 2/3. The number of officials almost doubled.

Parkinson's book became a best seller and is often laughed at, but the work was dead serious – and meant to suggest a fundamental flaw in most organizations. Parkinson noted that "an official wants to multiply subordinates, not rivals" and that "officials make work for each other". For example, suppose you work in a large organization, and you wish to gain rank. To do so, the optimal strategy is to hire not one but two people underneath you to delegate tasks to. Having these two reports give you a team to manage – and instant prestige as a "manager" within the organization. It elevates you to a superior status to a rival with a single direct report, or worse, without any reports at all.

The result of this tendency for growth is, according to Parkinson, that any bureaucracy will grow at 5-7% per year, completely "irrespective of any variation of the amount of work to be done".

Parkinson's Law, as Gorbachev himself noted[3], is universal. Bureaucracies on their own accord grow, and, like a complex plant with a deep root-system, become close to impossible to uproot. None of the players in the political system have an incentive to shrink government, or in any way tie its growth to objective measures – such as the overall size of the economy.

Olson's Law

While Parkinson's law provides a basis for spontaneous growth of organizations such as federal and state governments, another law is at work which encourages the complexity of the laws these governments enact. That law, clearly identified by the economist Mancur Olson in 1965, is that small interest groups always yield disproportionate power in democratic societies.

Take any well organized, narrow interest group such as the National Rifle Association, the American Association of Retired People, or the Corn Growers Association. Each of these groups will have specific demands of government: keep firearms legal, maintain social security, keep farm subsidies. Each one of them can promise to withhold a substantial number of votes in any general election in which these demands are not met.

With most elections fought in the center, these swing votes are critical. This is why that even Democrats who, in private are for gun control, relent in public to not lose the NRA vote. Or why Republicans, who ideally want to keep overall government expenditures down, vote like Bush did, in favor of a massive increase in prescription drug benefits.

There are now so many special interest groups, with so many different agendas, that it takes huge staffs of strategists to figure out how to optimally address them in an election year. Politics becomes a game of three dimensional chess, where the correct position is to be "for many things, and against very few[4]" to quote one of Lyndon Johnson's campaign slogans. (in contrast, Bernard Baruch once opined "vote for the man who promises the least, because he will be the least likely to disappoint"[5]).

Note that ceding to special interests usually means growing the budgets in ways that don't correspond to any clear economic need. Why subsidize the production of ethanol? Because there are significant numbers of corn farmers who will vote against you if you don't. Why spend enormous sums on veteran pensions? Because there are a lot of voting veterans.

Pandering to any specific cause will not cause a mass uproar in the general population. Spread across three hundred million people, the impact of corn subsidies are negligible – maybe five dollars per person per year. But multiplied across all the different types of special interests, this effect is very real.

As government becomes more and more complex, Olson's law has a more profound influence. With few laws on the statutes, it was probably very difficult to pass clear special interest legislation in early America. However, as the complexity of the overall system grows, it is easier and easier to hide this type of vote buying. Nobody can follow every piece of legislation; complex bills such as the Obama TARP bill can include hundreds of items designed to placate special interests.

In his seminal book The Rise and Decline of Nations[6], Olson makes an extremely convincing case that the cartelization of any stable economic system will only grow over time, and that nothing short of a major revolution (or war) will cause a reboot. Countries emerging from major war damage, such as France, Germany and Japan post WW2, tend to grow faster. Newer settled states such as Texas and California have higher growth rates than older states such as New York or Ohio.

This effect is entirely due entirely to game-theory incentives which push some players in the economic system to seek advantage for themselves at the expense of the common good. It is as if sooner or later, a stable government will give rise to fragmented "prisoner dilemma" type behavior, where wage floors, tariffs, import restrictions, subsidies and other completely non-economic effects set in.

The parallel with software development is exact. In older software projects the code becomes rigid and archaic. Changes become very difficult. Complexity sets in and takes root.

Eventually growth slows to a halt, and a complete re-write must be undertaken. Once that re-write occurs, growth accelerates again.

Baumol's Law

In the 1960's the economist William Baumol described a phenomena[7] where wages can increase even when labor productivity does not. An example of this would be the salary of a classical musician. Even though "it always takes 4 people to form a string quartet", salaries of each of the players can rise, as their alternative money making options increases (with a growing economy).

In many cases, running a government *seems* to require a large amount of people: soldiers, schoolteachers, police force etc.... At the scale of the United States, this inherently large number of people works in the favor of more complexity and more cost. As we will see below, an astonishing 17 million people work for state and local governments; technology has *so far* done little to reduce that number or contain their pay levels.

The key word here is *so far*. Things are changing – quickly. In education, online courses are offering an alterative to massive amounts of schoolteachers. Better websites and apps are replacing telephone help hotlines at all levels of government. Drones and electronic warfare are replacing soldiers. The idea of a huge percentage of the countries population working for the state is a 20th century concept.

Machiavelli's Law

Machiavelli famously chronicled the use and abuse of power in renaissance Italy. "Absolute Power" he said, "corrupts absolutely." Today, the economic power wielded by top government officials in the US, Russia and China far exceeds that of the Medici's even after fully adjusting for Inflation. In all three cases – including the United States – corruption in its many forms and flavors runs wild.

In the US, this starts in congress. Not only can special interest groups influence legislation by pledging or withholding votes, they also do so with cold hard cash – in the form of campaign contributions, political action committee contributions and other "scratch my back and I will scratch yours" contributions. The HBO Series "House of Cards" with Kevin Spacey was an instant success for dramatizing these dealings, which are a fact of everyday life on Capitol Hill.

Congress, as they say, "is for sale", and because of laws on campaign contributions, the price is, paradoxically, quite low. Any new special interest group can get access to the government at the cost of a few well paid lobbyists. Companies such as Verizon or Northrop Grumman have thousands, infiltrating every layer of the system looking for legislative angles to support their agendas.

Hiring ex-government officials in top business posts is now standard practice. Shultz, who ran the Defense department under Reagan, retired to Bechtel, a significant Defense contractor. Paul Volker, chairman of the federal Reserve was hired by Wasserstein Perella, a top investment bank. Dick Cheney, the Vice President under Bush moved from Halliburton to the White House and back to Halliburton.

None of this is (yet) illegal. If you run a large aerospace defense company, you want to ensure you have as many ex-generals in your employ as money can buy. Not only are they on a first name basis with the people making the ultimate procurement decisions, they stand as a monument to where those same people will go once they make the "right choices."

The same is true in banking. The placement of key people in government positions will give your firm an advantage over other banks in times of difficulty. The cozy relationship between Goldman Sachs and both G. W. Bush's and Obama's administration has been well documented by Matt Taiebi of Rolling Stone Magazine. In 2008, Goldman was one the key contributors to the financial crisis; not only did the firm escape with very few fines, they were given large responsibilities in the bailout phase that followed. Bear Stearns, with fewer ties to Washington was not so lucky.

The Fallacy of Central Planning

The fourth and probably most significant reason that government is complex is the flawed thinking that central planning actually works.

This is a tricky subject, which we will deal with in much greater detail later. But the key thought here is as follows: one of the main reasons that government is big, is that many people actually still believe that bigger is better.

The naïve thinking goes a bit like this: we clearly have a lot of problems in area X (healthcare, education, jobs, welfare benefits, the environment etc..). The answer has to be to give the government more resources to deal with X. We have no idea how the government actually will address this, but the general the idea of "spending more money there" seems like a sound one. Politicians run with these ideas, get elected, and then build up departments underneath them – but area X remains an issue. The supposed cure – more money, more government, more central planning – simply doesn't work. In fact, in many cases, it perversely has the opposite effect: healthcare and education quality goes down, unemployment goes up etc..

The idea of central planning *seems* good. If the country can mobilize to put a man on the moon, how come it can't provide decent healthcare and a decent wage to every American? These are great goals and, we believe, quite achievable – but the way to achieve them is not by brute force government decree.

In the Chapter 5 we will discuss *why* central planning is generally doomed to failure, but for now lets consider the abysmal track record of the approach overall. Over the last 100 years, almost every single country has implemented some variant of central planning to promote the continued welfare of its citizens. In every single case, the results have been far from ideal.

The most extreme examples: communist Russia, Cuba, China and North Korea were all unmitigated disasters. Government got very big, freedom went to zero, and the miraculous economic effects that were hoped for never materialized. India tried a more socialistic approach, emphasizing 5 year plans put together by teams of professional economists, together with currency controls and tariffs to protect the domestic economy. The results are in: Indians never gave up their freedom, but the infrastructure and economy of India is still third-world.

In western Europe, an all-encompassing welfare state was superimposed on a market economy. The result, in the case of France, is that over 50% of the economy now *is* the government (or works for it directly), and while some form of socialized healthcare has been achieved – it is at huge cost to the overall economy. Europe as a whole is in a deep recession with no easy way out.

Reasons for Complexity -- Summary

There are very good reasons why government is not simple, and why it getting more complicated by the day. As Yoda said in Star Wars, "Simple – Yes, Easy – No." Like an overgrown vine that has encircled an old house, our government has roots growing in every direction. It won't be a simple matter to clean it up. In fact, as Mancur Olson argues in *The Rise and Decline of Nations*, the only way out may be an outright revolution.

3. The Government as a Product.

LETS START BY APPROACHING GOVERNMENT AS IF IT WERE JUST ANOTHER PRODUCT. What does this product cost? What are its benefits? Is it a product that I can use right out of the box or do I need to read a long and complicated manual? Is the product well designed? Is it product that people (or companies) love?

If we for a moment ignore exactly how we got here, and focus on exactly what we would want our government to look like, a clearer picture emerges.

Great Products are Intuitive

A first quality of every great product is that it should immediately graspable. When the Sony Walkman first appeared in the 1980's it was a simple device with just a few buttons. It did not need a manual. 30 years later, the exact same thing can be said about the iPhone, Google or Uber. These products are simple and clear enough that, in Silicon Valley speech, "even your mother could use them."

The US government clearly does not pass that test. With a tax code that is so complex over 80% of Americans need help filling out their taxes, with our body of laws doubling in size every twenty years and with hundreds of welfare programs there is nothing remotely intuitive about our government.

To use a computer analogy, the government is like a bloated version of Microsoft Word. There are 6 toolbars, three spell checkers, and six ways to change a given formatting style. To figure the thing out you need a certified expert to come in and give you advice. Yes, there are a lot of features. No, they are not easily understood.

Great Products have Benefits that Exceed Costs

In 2009, according to a memo from the Joint Committee on Taxation, a bi-partisan Congressional committee, only 49 percent of Americans owed money on their federal income tax returns. So for about half of Americans, the product we are describing is actually close to free.

For the other 50 percent, the product is relatively expensive. That group pays 36% of its income to the federal government. On top of this, the tax paying group pays on average about 7% in state taxes and 6% in social security taxes – all told, about half of all earned income goes to some form of national or state government.

Now certainly, the benefits of living in America outweigh these high costs. But these benefits can hardly be tied to the government itself. As we will argue throughout this book, a much smaller government could provide the same services, or more, to the average person at a significantly lower cost. In fact, if a person could opt to get only 50% of the "benefits" of the government at a 50% lower tax rate, it is clear that most people would take that deal. If you could pay half your tax and get a military that is "only" 5 times as large as the next largest military and a welfare state that is "only" the same size as it was in 1990 wouldn't you do it?

John Stuart Mill genuinely asked himself whether people who paid no taxes should be allowed to vote. From a pure product perspective, that makes sense. Obviously, such a person would always prefer more benefits. On the other hand, if there is a cost to these benefits, presumably people will optimize the size of government accordingly.

Great Products are Competitive

Yahoo and Bing are good search engines. In a blind test, they rank very close to Google in terms of results. But they are not *as good* as Google, and at a free price point – consumers tend to pick Google by a wide margin. Pepsi is a decent cola. So is RC Cola. But most consumers prefer the taste of Coca Cola over either of them.

Even in the 1700's, Adam Smith realized that a man with his own capital had a choice as to where to deploy that capital.

This is one of the main reasons he was opposed to corporate taxes of any kind. Today, this choice is greater than ever for big multinationals to small entrepreneurs. A government that is pro-business, with relaxed labor laws, predictably low taxation, and reduced red tape will attract capital and ideas.

In the 60's and 70's only large multinational corporations could set up shop abroad. Today, it's a relatively simple process to set up a company in Singapore, Ireland or the British Virgin Islands. Workers can be hired on a contract basis in India, the Ukraine, or Argentina. Even if you are legally incorporated in the US, all your actual operations can be easily outsourced, meaning that you as an small business owner will not actually create jobs in the United States.

Individuals as well as business now have increasing options. Every point on the globe is no more than a 24 hour trip from every other point. English is increasingly a universal language. People with desirable skills, in science, engineering and medicine can easily relocate to a different country. Government is a big component of that choice. The weather in Liberia might be excellent, but the idea of living in a dictatorship run by a warlord has limited appeal. French wine and cheese may be the best in the world, but few people will choose to locate their startup to a country with a 70% capital gains tax rate, a 2% wealth tax, and draconian employment laws.

The United States is (still) an enviable place to live for many. On the other hand, as we will see later, many Chinese engineering graduates are now opting to move back to China after their education.

Great Services are Optional.

The mark of a truly great product or service is that you can leave it. The phrase "satisfaction guaranteed or your money back" comes to mind. If you buy an iPhone and you decide the next day that you don't want it, you can call Apple and return it. If you are not happy at Motel 6, your stay is on the house.

On the other hand, the US tax system is, for its citizens, a one way street. You can live abroad, but as a US citizen, you are still forced to pay US taxes. It's the only country in the world that taxes you globally. You can try to drop your citizenship, but there may be "exit taxes" to do so – and the government may never let you back in the country. Once you do this, an undocumented worker has more freedom to come and reside in America than you do.

The US is busy trying to make sure its millionaires don't leave the US, when in fact it should be trying its best to making sure it attracts foreign millionaires *into* the US. If you do in fact provide the best product on the market, you won't have to worry about people leaving. Some certainly will, but more will definitely come in.

Software companies now are starting to understand this. As much as Microsoft fought hard to get people into a proprietary one-way windows environment, it is now back peddling to try to make their systems more "open". Unfortunately for them, its too late. The brand of Microsoft, like the brand of Facebook will be forever branded as roach motels – you can check in, but you can't check out.

Great Products have Good Websites

Twenty years ago, most products shipped with long instruction manuals, often printed in multiple languages. For software products, the sheer size of these instruction manuals was perceived as an indication of value – I remember distinctly the manual for Adobe Photoshop 3.0 which was well over a thousand pages thick.

Today, instruction manuals are obsolete. What is important is that there is a source of information, freely accessible, on the web. That information is not only static – it is an actual information product, personalized to the user, and delivered openly over the world wide web, and via apps.

There should be a login. Right now you have a login to your Bank, your Google account, your Apple account, your Facebook account. There is no login to your account at the US government. We need a way to login, change your address if you move, view your taxes, pay your taxes, check your retirement and medical benefits and actually vote.

Your carbon footprint, your taxable wages, documentation on any proposed laws, explanation of the penalties for not following the laws – all of these should be online. Customer support, in the form of phone and online chat should be available 24 hours a day, seven days a week.

Great Products are Sustainable

Remember Bernie Madoff? The NY "financial genius" had the top selling product in the entire hedge fund world, an investment that returned double digits year in and year out with clockwork regularity. Except of course, it wasn't sustainable. Madoff was found to be cooking the books, and everybody who invested with him suffered huge losses.

The US government, as well as most other worldwide governments at this time shows alarming similarities with Madoff's ponzi scheme. Our debt is approaching limits that any sane observer would regard as toxic. Deficits relative to GDP are reaching new heights. And, like Madoff, our accounting is shady.

For our government to be truly sustainable, the Budget should be balanced. Not sometime in the future, but now and for ever more. There needs to be strict controls to prevent the government from spending more than it brings in. And the solution should not be "tax more". A simple flat tax should be all that the government gets, and its should live off that amount, exactly.

The federal government should have a clear, simplified accounting rules. There should be no "off budget" items like Homeland security, or Social Security. It should be absolutely clear where the spending is taking place.

Defense Spending should be targeted to a reasonable percentage of our GDP. It is not acceptable that in 2010 we spent almost 100% of all income tax receipts on Defense and Defense-related activities – including veterans benefits. We do need a strong defense, but unless there is a genuine war, the spend should fall inside clearly defined quantitative bounds.

Great Products are Predictable

The great iconic designs of the twentieth century – the Porsche cabriolet, the Eames chair, the Rolex submariner, the Gucci loafer, the Boeing 747 have not changed much at their core. In some cases, they have evolved – but the evolution has been progressive and predictable. Even in the fast changing world of computers, the keyboard shortcuts for the Apple Macintosh have stayed consistent for over 40 years.

There is huge value in keeping products predictable. One of the huge mistakes Microsoft made with Vista and later with Windows 8, was to dramatically change the user interface, requiring hundreds of millions of users to learn new ways to do the same things.

Our government is guilty of exactly this kind of crime. Tax rates are lowered, then raised, then lowered – all in a very unpredictable fashion. In the decision to start a company or not, we can only guess what the tax will be on capital gains if we sell it some time in the future.

Healthcare policy keeps changing every few years. We don't understand what medical insurance costs will be for our employees. We don't understand how the regulatory environment could change against us.

Social security is technically bankrupt, but the issue is not being addressed head on. At some point in the not-to-distant future, many are going to face a rude awakening when the retirement they thought was coming to them isn't.

As we will argue again and again, taxes should be clear, simple, and should not change. I will argue further in the book that an overall 20% income tax rate – payable only by individuals, and an elimination of the social security tax and capital gains tax should be enough to pay our bills. Everybody, including low income workers can afford to pay this tax.

Clear policies must be developed with respect to the Government bailing out banks and other financial institutions. We cannot have a repeat of 2009, where the US almost led the world into a financial Armageddon. We cannot have any more "extra-ordinary" bailouts.

Great Products are Ubiquitous

The Lamborghini Countache is certainly an excellent product, but with a price tag of a quarter of a million dollars, is it really great? The truly "insanely great" aspect of the Macintosh (and later the iPhone) is that it is truly a device of the people. Workers in China, who can't afford computers have iPhones. Kids in sub-Saharan Africa use Google. Now that's greatness.

Our government needs to address all classes of society, including the bottom third. That does not mean a "welfare state" – but it does mean a safety net, that encourages individuals to "pick themselves up" and find jobs.

There should be a simplified system of near-free medical healthcare for everybody, administered at the national level, with a choice of service providers and an upgrade path. Patients should be able to choose more expensive treatments, but the state should only cover part of that. Even for basic treatment, patients should be encouraged to shop around, and they should benefit from choosing more cost effective options. The government should sponsor wellness and fitness as well as cover the cost of disease treatment.

There needs to be some level of support to people who make very low salaries, or who are retired and living off a very low income. They should still pay taxes (on what salaries they do make), but they should also get some basic stipend. In all cases, they should be incentivized to work more to make more money than the base amount.

The government should do more to offer choice incentivize education. Online education works. There should be money available to everybody who hits measurable thresholds. National testing centers should be set up to test in a wide variety of areas: math, science, language skills, sales, medical skills, etc. Online certificates (with distinctions) should be awarded to people who pass the tests; and actual cash money should paid.

Government as a Product – Summary

If you were to design the government from scratch today, you certainly would not end up with what we have. You would have something far simpler, more predictable, cheaper, with a much better cost benefit ratio. It would address all aspects of society, but would encourage employment, not dependence on the welfare state. It would also encourage immigration, and would not prohibit emigration. And finally, it would have a clean, useful web interface.

4. A Simple Web Interface

Your Account at USA.gov

ONE OF THE FIRST THINGS EVERY STARTUP COMPANY IN SILICON VALLEY DOES is implement a web login. For most companies this is no more than a username (or email) and a password. For more secure operations, such as financial applications, two factor authentication is generally enabled – a unique code is sent to your cell phone for example, which needs to be keyed in to get access.

Once logged in, every new application needs, at a minimum a place to change your name and address, set your email alert preferences, and change your email and password.

Amazingly, our federal government still doesn't have a central login. We all have a unique identifier (our social security numbers or corporate employer numbers), but these are not directly tied to a central online account. This needs to change. If Startups can do it, the 3 Trillion a year enterprise known as the USA can do it as well.

www.usa.gov is US government's official web portal. The site contains an assortment of random information (for example,

"Find new, seized, and surplus cars, houses and more"), and the ability to "follow it" on Facebook and Twitter, but there is no area for a user to create an account or login.

Figure 1 The Actual US Government Web Portal as of June, 2014.

The website design, information organization and attention to detail on this website portal is on par with a typical DMV office. The Facebook page and blog page (yes, the United States actually has a blog) are worse. For example, as I am writing this, the Facebook page only had 270,000 "likes" (an extremely low number for a site like this), and was last updated 13 hours ago.

Still, according to the measurement service Quantcast[8], usa.gov still manages to get 5,000,000 unique visitors a month – making it the 282nd most viewed site on the entire web. If you add in all the traffic from the state portals (ny.gov itself gets 2,500,000 unique visitors) – there are probably 20,000,000 people a month who visit some form of government portal – or about one adult American in ten. This is very real traffic, and show that people *want* to online access. It should give people in Washington (and in the state Capitols) a sense of the huge opportunity there is for e-government.

A Single Login for Federal, State and Local

People don't like to have to remember multiple accounts and passwords. This is one of the reasons why "Login with Facebook" buttons have permeated the web. For security and continuity reasons, the government needs its own login – it can't rely on a third party such as Facebook or Google – but there is no reason for each state and city to have their own account systems.

People move and they expect their data to move with them. Just because I cross the Hudson from New Jersey to New York, shouldn't mean that I have to start over with a new account at ny.gov, the portal of the state of NY (which gets 2.3 million visitors a month on its own). I want a single login for all my data: federal, state and local.

Having a common login doesn't mean that this effort *has* be coordinated across the 50 states, or thousands of local governments. However, having a consistent user interface for paying your taxes, voting, and retrieving information is a *good thing*. With all due respect to the different efforts behind the web design teams of ca.gov, ny.gov, etc.., the core information there can be presented in a consistent (and better looking, more intuitive) fashion across all states, and all localities.

It Should be Beautiful

It's easy to roll your eyes and say "this is just design, it's not really important." But Apple (and others) have taught us that user interface and design really matter. People interact with good looking, well designed products in a completely different way than they do with ugly, poorly designed ones. Again, thinking about the government as a product – one of the first considerations is that it should be beautiful.

Any new startup pitching for funding on Sand Hill Road in Silicon Valley knows this. While products like MySpace could get funded in 2005, the standards are higher today. Every single company that Sequoia Capital has funded in the last 5 years has a gorgeous, industrial-design quality website. And it's not particularly expensive. At this point, quality web service design is a known art – and a few good designers can create pixel-ready concepts for something like this in just weeks. A high-end design shop such as Ideo could create a thing of beauty.

Paying and Reviewing Your Taxes Online

One of the first, albeit unpleasant, functions of your new account at usa.gov should be looking up what taxes are due, paying them, and reviewing records of past payments.

As I will discuss in Chapter 6, I think there are very strong arguments for dramatically simplifying the tax structure to the point where a person can file their taxes, by themselves, in just a few minutes. Regardless of whether this is adopted, the taxes section of your account at usa.gov should show a breakdown of what the government believes you owe, and a facility for paying it.

In a flat tax scenario, this boils down to enumerating all the sources of income for the year and multiplying by the flat tax rate. Some of these income figures can be pre-filled as the government collects this information from employers on the fly – and can be then edited by the user if inaccurate.

A single interface should be provided, ideally, for federal, state and local governments. This way, a user could review a statement for example, of 2020 when he or she was a resident of New York City, with NY state taxes and NYC taxes – side by side with a statement from 2021 when that same person moved to California.

Accessing and reviewing past information might end up being as beneficial as facilitating payment. Having personally just gone through a divorce, I can attest to the difficulty of obtaining past tax documents from the US and California governments. Having this information readily available, in a consistent format for planning purposes would be very desirable.

And finally, there is the payment itself. The government could offer direct deposit (see section), payment by credit card, and could potentially offer credit terms for people who are in a cash crunch. The idea of the IRS as a loan shark may seem a little odd, but in point of fact, this is exactly how they operate right now – with double digit fees and penalties, that are imposed retroactively with very little transparency. It might be a good idea to make these fees more explicit, and give people an option to pay more, later as opposed to the smaller amount today.

Your Money at the Fed

I believe that it would beneficial for individuals to be able to store money, in the form of cash deposits, with the Federal Reserve. Unlike banks, which ultimately only have a partial guarantee by the FDIC (a guarantee up to $100,000, and a guarantee of ultimate repayment, not of timely repayment), money at the Fed would be as good as the Federal Reserve itself, in other words as good as cash.

Your account at the Fed could be fully electronic, and transferable to another individual or company, just like Bitcoin, at zero cost. Ultimately this could replace cash banknotes entirely. In the interim, it could be accessed just like any other banking deposit at any ATM machine worldwide. Disbursement could be made in any local currency – just as today with deposits held at a commercial bank.

Opening an account with the Federal Reserve (or with other central banks who follow this scheme) would be open to all individuals of all nationalities, and to companies. So if I wanted to transfer money to another individual in France, I could do so immediately with this system, and the money would be instantly available to that person (assuming he or she also had an account). That person could then go to an ATM and withdraw the cash in euros.

This secure e-cash would be a boon for the economy, as it could fulfill the early promise of Bitcoin as a method of electronic payment, but avoid the wild fluctuations in its value. Indeed, Bitcoin (and other crypto-currencies) have no intrinsic value and, while the same can be said for the US dollar in a philosophical sense, in a practical sense the value of the dollar does not change much over a span of a few years.

Also, unlike Bitcoin, transfers could be authoritatively confirmed in real time. A secure login to your account at the Federal Reserve could immediately confirm to you that in fact a transfer has taken place, and where it came from (unlike wire transfers, where the identity of the sender is often hard to decipher). The register of transaction at the Fed could also be used in the case of legal dispute to show that payment in fact did take place. This could add a level of security to transactions that Bitcoin could never have (try explaining to a judge that you paid a certain individual 10 bitcoins for a bike that you never received – there is no authoritative record that you ever owned the 10 Bitcoins in the first place).

People may wonder if this will in some sense encourage money laundering or other illicit activities. My answer is that it is far easier, and less traceable to use cash, diamonds, or even Bitcoins for such dealings. Having a complete record of every one of your transactions at the US government is not, for a criminal, an ideal proposition.

In any case, if this proposal is adapted, your account at usa.gov would be the natural place to review your transactions and balance, transfer money, and use balances that you may have on hand to instantly pay your taxes. You would be notified via text or email that the payment was due, when the funds are received, and when any suspicious activity to your account occurred (access from a different country, change of email address etc..)

Of course such as system would have to be secure. But we now have tens of thousands of banks who have successfully implemented online banking; our collective experience in this area is vast, and improving every year. Different security options could be offered to users including biometric scanning (retina scan or fingerprints), IP whitelisting (transfers can only be made from certain designated locations), two factor authentication (login requires confirming a code sent to a cell phone or key fob) and so on. Limits on transfer size, automatic freezing of accounts after x logins and so on could be set by users, and made difficult to change remotely. In general, security should not be an issue in 2014.

Voting

Once we have a secure, unique ID for every person, we can also allow voting on the Internet. We already allow voting by mail; this would be far more secure, and significantly more convenient.

Economic studies have shown that voter turnout is a function of both the perceived benefits of voting (especially high in tightly contested elections), and in the costs to the voters. This applies not only to presidential elections (where voter turnout is on an upswing with 57% participation in the 2008 and 2012 elections vs. a low of 49% in 1996), but also to state and local elections. By making a common voting technology available to federal, state and local elections, we could greatly increase citizen engagement at all levels of the government.

As with the game "Who Wants to be a Millionaire", this technology could be also useful for a number of polling activities outside the strict 4 year election cycle. For example, people could provide feedback in the form of "like" or "dislike" on specific pieces of legislation.

Your Medical Records and Benefits

One of the key proposals I will make in Chapter 11, is that an effort should be made to centralize medical records into a single database that patients can access with them no matter what state they live in, or what doctor they see.

These medical records could be entirely private, or you could elect to share some or all of them with a doctor / trainer / nutritionist etc.. Or, entirely at your option, you could share them with a private insurance company of your choosing.

A second part of the healthcare proposals I will make in Chapter 8 is for a basic minimal universal healthcare coverage, whose benefits can be applied towards more expensive, private treatment – where you pick the service provider.

Your personal medical visit data might look like this

Date	Operation	Cost	Coverage
Jan 21, 2019	Blood work Panel	$200	$195
Jan 19, 2019	Chest X Ray	$356	$351
Jan 10, 2019	MRI	$2000	$1500
Jan 3, 2019	Annual Exam Bonus		$300

Figure 2 Individual Medical Data, Aggregated at the National Level.

In this example the Jan 21 and Jan 19 visits were covered up to a small $5 deductible. The Jan 10 MRI operation was only covered up to $1,500 – the patient elected to go for a premium service provider. On Jan 3, the patient successfully passed an annual health exam and was granted a $300 bonus for exceptional health – and a badge to prove it. As mentioned in the first chapter, I believe that rewarding people for good behavior could be a key part of the "gamification" of health and e-government. This will be further discussed in Chapter 8.

Other Government Programs

There are numerous other governmental programs and services on the federal, state and local levels that could benefit from the universal Government login

- The Global Entry, Sentri and TSA Pre programs that allow automatic pre-screening for passing borders and avoiding lines.

- The ability to order new passports, birth certificates, or state ID cards.

- Information and Enrollment in the Armed Forces, Peace Corps or Military Reserves.

- Ability to apply for visas for foreign travel.

- Tie in with the state DMV records to renew registration and licenses, get driving sample tests etc..

- Tie in with state property tax databases to review and pay your property taxes.

- Tie in with local and national crime prevention programs.

The list could end up getting very long. They key is a single database, with a single login. This could start out small and evolve over time.

Local Government Tie In

A number of state government services could be tied in to usa.gov. Want to report a pothole or an environmental hazard? Your usa.gov account would be the first place to look. Want to get notified about the fires 100 miles away? Sign up for fire alerts under the "state" tab. Have a strong opinion on the new library they are planning to put in at the corner of Main and Elm? Leave your comment and be heard. Need to pay a parking ticket? You know where to go.

Local government participation has been tried by private companies, but getting any kind of critical mass has been difficult. Govworks.com was one attempt profiled in the movie startup.com, but was ultimately unsuccessful, closing shop in 2001. 13 years later, the government itself could and should try it again. Especially by combining federal, state and local in a single focal point would almost guarantee critical mass. And, unlike private attempts this could remain a (relatively small) cost center for ever – no need to turn a profit by advertising or subscription revenue.

A Coordinated Series of Apps

The US government has barely scratched the surface on what it can do on the web, at a time when the web itself is being left in the dust by mobile apps. Companies like Facebook, Twitter and Google are now seeing most of their traffic coming from iOS or Android devices, on either smart phones or tablets. The government has the very beginnings of an app strategy, but these it's a sad start.

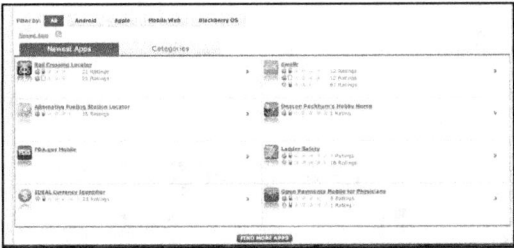

Figure 3 The US government's attempt at apps. Note the ratings

A much better strategy would be to hire a design firm (such as IDEO) and develop a consistent branded family of apps, with a common design language – and of course using the common US government login.

These apps would be designed and paid for by the federal government, and provided free of charge to state and local authorities. The cost would be minimal on a national scale, and would allow even poor municipalities to take advantage of this new technology. It would also give all Americans a consistent user interface regardless of where they live, move or travel in the 50 states.

Uber for The Police and Fire

In many towns, including my hometown of Los Angeles, the Police are busy arresting Uber drivers for, among other sins, taking perfectly willing customers to the airport. A better use of their time, and of taxpayers money, would be to embrace the Uber technology themselves. The simple idea of seeing –

on a map – all available cars, and later, tracking the car you call could be applied perfectly to the police force, the fire department, and to emergency medical help.

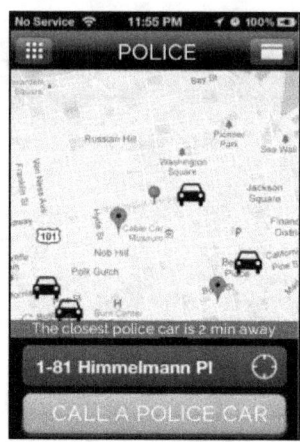

Figure 4 Uber For Police.

Imagine clicking one button on an app to dispatch a police car. Another one to call or chat with the officer as he or she makes his way to you. And, vice versa, imagine it from the police officer's perspective: instead of a random voice at the end of the line, the officer could quickly review your file, quickly ascertain if the request is serious, and use that data to coordinate the best possible response.

With data comes power. If the majority of police and fire requests come via online or through an app, that data could be used to better plan increases or reductions in the force, or distribution of officers from one geographical area to another. Key Performance Indicators (KPIs) – such as the mean time to respond to an incident and the rating of individual officers and overall satisfaction levels – could be used to quantitatively assess and improve police and fire units nationwide.

Maps for Buses, Public Works, Emergencies

Police, fire departments and emergency medical services could all benefit from a single "push to dispatch" buttons. But other services could take advantage of a simple map presentation – without the contact button. For example, in Santa Monica, where I currently live, I would like to be able to see, on a map the following:

- location of every single bus, with the ability to search for an individual bus by line or destination

- road closures – with the ability to click and find out more details. Is highway one closed for a bike race? How long is it expected to stay closed? Is there someone I can chat with or talk to in real time?

- Location of libraries, parks and other public facilities.

- Emergency information. Having lived through two major Malibu fires, I would have loved an app which showed the progression of fires, evacuation routes etc..

It is true that companies like Google and Yahoo have *some* of this information, but without a system designed for local government, where government can input data in real time, and retrieve that data post-fact for analysis, very little can be achieved.

Getting Help And Providing Feedback

Usa.gov could be your first stop to getting real time help by chat or voice on any topic. Have a question on your income tax? Ask a specialist. Want to understand your retirement benefits better? Chat with someone who can help you. Instead of repeating your name and situation each time, you could share all, or part of your file with a cleared specialist.

The interface for this app would be very similar to Skype. Records of each conversation would be kept for future use. Unclear about what someone in the housing permits section was saying? Consult the chat log. Forgot which road was closed? Instead of calling again, simply re-read the chat conversation.

And getting help is only one side of the coin. The other one is reporting problems and providing feedback on all elements of state, local and even federal government. Have a better idea of what to do with the empty lot next to the library that is shutting down? Submit your request – either privately, or on a public forum. Want to complain about an individual police officer or other public servant? There should be a simple way to submit a complaint – and have that complaint immediately go to the right department.

The entire process of e-government itself could be designed in a public feedback loop. Engineers, artists, designers, teachers, technologists, and just regular citizens could all collaborate to improve the overall process – by submitted their ideas to public forums, by creating ad-hoc working groups around key issues, and by giving feedback on the existing state of the system.

A Simple Web Interface – Summary.

One of the simplest, and most obvious fixes to the "system" that is that there be a centralized "account" at the US government where you could vote, pay taxes and potentially even deposit money, among other activities. It could start out small, but end up become a true software as a service system – perhaps eventually the single most important such system in the world.

Although the system should be designed and paid for by the federal government, hooks should be put in place for state and local authorities to use the system at a more granular level, allowing for example an "uber for police" and "uber for fire" capabilities, among others. The system could also be used to provide feedback on how well government is working in general, and specifically which public servants are doing a good job and which ones are not.

Technology has progressed tremendously over the last 20 years. The government has not been a big participant in that change. It's time to bring our core systems up to current standards.

5. Economics Simplified

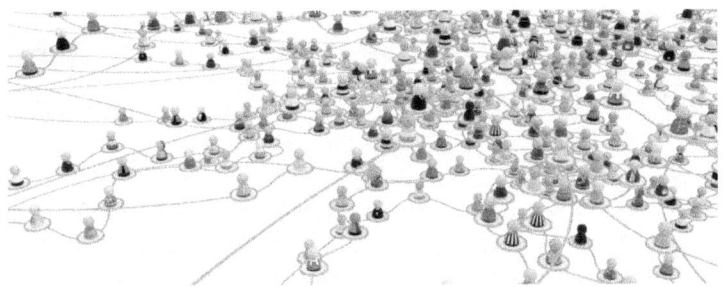

Economies are Networks

BEFORE WE GET MUCH FURTHER, IT IS TIME WE ASK OURSELVES: "WHAT IS AN ECONOMY?" How does one actually begin to think about something as complex as the United States economy, or, for that matter a smaller economy such as Iceland?

One good way is to think about them as *networks*. There are two kinds of nodes in an economic network: individuals and companies. These nodes are connected to each other if one node provides a product or service to another node.

In the case of the United States, there are about 300 million individuals and about 10 million businesses (mainly small businesses) that comprise the nodes of the network. Most individuals provide their services to a single employer, although some service providers (gardeners, maids, repairmen etc..) have connections to multiple other nodes.

Companies have outgoing connections to every individual and every other company that consumes their product. Amazon.com and Wal-Mart touch tens of millions of nodes in the network. The barbershop on Main Street in Appleton Wisconsin touches a hundred or less.

In this network new links are formed at every moment of every day. Companies decide to stop using supplier X and instead switch to supplier Y. Individuals decide to try out the new barbershop on Elm Street, instead of Main Street where they usually go. Companies hire and fire. Individuals have children, die, go broke and occasionally win the lottery.

The visual image you should now have in your head is somewhat similar to the human brain. Ignoring even the fact that a company or individual can have more than one product or supply more than one service, the number of combinations is on the order of 300 million squared or 90,000,000,000,000,000 (90 quadrillion). This is approximately the same number of atoms in a human body.

Now how do market economies work? Or how (absent government control) *should* they work? The answer is using *prices* as the key signal for link creation and destruction.

Consider a typical small business, supplying say accounting services to a local community. It can lower the price of its services and gain more market share, but this hurts profits. If the rent on its offices goes up, its profits will suffer, and it may have to move. If the prospect for profits are good it will hire more staff. If they are bad, they will cut staff.

That individual node is therefore taking account all the price information from nodes that it could do business with and uses this price information to set its own prices on the products or services that it produces. It's a process where, like the brain, every single node in the network is adjusting in real time to price signals from hundreds, thousands or even millions of other nodes.

This system, like human brains, actually works. One of the first people to recognize it was the Scottish economist Adam Smith, who published his observations in 1776 in the classic "Wealth of Nations.[9]" Co-incidentally, this was the also birthdate of the first modern democracy, the United States of America.

Economics is Not A Science

The point of the network metaphor is that economic systems are by, their very nature, complex – and resist simplification. The possible network organization patterns at any single point for an economy like the United States are in the quadrillions. And these change every day – as every participant in the network re-assesses their pricing, their suppliers, who are they selling to and how they feel. Random variables, such as what a CEO had for breakfast, actually matter.

For the last hundred years this has not stopped the academic community from trying to "model" entire economies as sets of equations. In fact, until very recently, you could not get a paper published in an Economic Journal unless there was some mathematical formula such as this one:

$$C_{g,t} = \frac{\delta' L_{f,t} w_{f,t}}{1+\beta^{\frac{1}{\sigma}} \left(\frac{\pi_{f,t+1}}{(1+r_{f,t})}\right)^{1-\frac{1}{\sigma}} \left(\frac{q_{t+1}}{q_t}\right)^{\frac{(1-\delta')(1-\sigma)}{\sigma}}} \qquad (4.35)$$

$$C_{\beta,t} = \frac{(1-\delta')L_{f,t} w_{f,t}}{\frac{1}{q_t} + \beta'^{\frac{1}{\sigma'}} \frac{1}{q_t}\left(\frac{\pi_{f,t+1}}{(1+r_{f,t})}\right)^{1-\frac{1}{\sigma'}}\left(\frac{q_{t+1}}{q_t}\right)^{\frac{(1-\delta')(1-\sigma')}{\sigma'}}} \qquad (4.36)$$

$$C_{g,2t+1} = \frac{\delta' L_{f,t} w_{f,t}}{\frac{\pi_{f,t+1}}{(1+r_{f,t})} + \beta'^{-\frac{1}{\sigma'}}\left(\frac{\pi_{f,t+1}}{(1+r_{f,t})}\right)^{\frac{1}{\sigma'}}\left(\frac{q_{t+1}}{q_t}\right)^{\frac{(1-\delta')(\sigma'-1)}{\sigma'}}} \qquad (4.37)$$

Figure 5 Example from mathematical economics, a field completely removed from the real world

These theories are only "true" in the sense that their assumptions reflect the reality of some world, present, past or future. For example, they assume that individuals are trying to "maximize" some form of "utility function", that economies somehow tend to "general equilibriums", and that highly oversimplified "econometric models" can be used to quantitatively predict economic outcomes.

As crazy as this now sounds (with the 2009 crisis behind us) it is worth remembering that many of the key economic decisions of the 20th century were in part influenced by theorists trying to extrapolate such highly abstract equations into recommendations on how to run the country. John Maynard

Keynes, in particular, was one of the biggest abusers of mathematics to advance his cause of bigger government. Today people speak of "Keysian ideas", but the actual mathematical economics that these ideas are based on has been quietly forgotten — and does not hold up well to the test of time.

In fact, more recent thinking, in particular by the Economist Robert Schiller of Yale[10], and by Kahneman and Tversky[11], has emphasized the much greater role of psychology in economic decisions. People, for example, buy stocks, simply because they are going up, not because they are discounting future dividends using some utility model. They stop working because they get discouraged. They are happy, not because of what they have, but of how much they have relative to other people, and relative to how much they used to have.

Psychology is not an "extra" thing to consider -- it's at the very core of how the economic network works. And making observations on psychology and human behavior is one of the areas where some economists have made, in my opinion, their greatest contributions. One of them, whose name is well known, but who is rarely read anymore is Milton Friedman.

Friedman was a traditional economist, who like others, spent most of his time concocting mathematical models of the economy that have long stopped being considered. He was however, also a quite practical person, who made a number of simple, but accurate observations on economic behavior that did have a very real impact — via Ronald Reagan. These ideas were laid out in a 10 part PBS series[12] called "Free to

Choose" that is freely available on YouTube, and in a book that was written after the series, that goes into greater detail.

If there is a future President of the United States reading this, I would encourage him or her to spend a few hours in an armchair absorbing Friedman's ideas. They apply equally well today as they did in 1980.

Milton Friedman's Matrix

One of key Friedman ideas is that individuals make their own choices very differently than the choices made by government planners on the part of individuals. He summarizes this in a following thought experiment, where you are asked to spend to your own money, or somebody else's money on either yourself or somebody else. This is what I call the "Friedman Matrix"

	For Me	For Somebody Else
My Money	1	2
Somebody Else's Money	3	4

In the first quadrant, you are spending your own money on yourself. In this case you are very concerned with both the price you are paying and the product or service you are getting. This is the natural state for nodes in the "Adam Smith / Free Market" network.

In the second quadrant you are spending your own money, but this time not on yourself – for example, on a gift for a loved one or business associate. In this case you are still likely to be very careful on how much you are spending, but generally somewhat less discerning on the quality of the good or service itself. After all – its not for you!

In the third quadrant, you are given money to spend on yourself. In this case, your incentive is to indulge. You will try to consume as much as possible, and to increase your spending limit as much as possible. This is for example the behavior of a healthcare patient with 100% free healthcare. Why not go back to the doctor for a visit if the visit is free? Why not get the extra vitamins? Why not consider cosmetic surgery if it is covered?

The final quadrant is where you are spending somebody else's money for somebody else. This is the case for a government employee – for example, a person designing a government railway website, or a congressman voting on a bridge in Alaska to win some votes in that district. In this case neither price nor quality of the product or service is of paramount importance. You can overpay, or deliver an inferior product without any immediate consequence.

Government Projects vs. Private Enterprise

Friedman's Matrix is at the core of why many government projects are so badly managed – the people in charge of those projects, at every level of execution, often have very little incentive to do better. Undoubtedly, the same can be said for many large corporations – but with one difference: companies are ultimately held responsible by their shareholders, where governments typically are not.

Let's consider an example of a government run steel company, such as British Steel pre-1980, and a private steel operation. The government run company has employees that are very difficult to fire. As long as they actually show up for work, they will tend to get automatic "performance raises" year after year. If the company as a whole is not doing well, the government will advance it more money. If it is having trouble competing with foreign steel companies, the government will institute tariffs to "protect domestic jobs." And, because they can't be replaced, if they are really unhappy, they can easily strike against the hand that feeds them, like the French rail workers are doing at the time I am writing this.

As a counter-point, consider the innovation of a small, up-start company called Nucor Steel – which arose from close to nothing to becoming America's top Steel Producer. With no government assistance, and very little resources, this company innovated out of necessity, pioneering the modern "minimill" concept[13]. That trajectory is inconceivable for a government run enterprise.

Historically, most governments have a bright example or two of projects that seem to be clear successes. For the US, it was the mobilization of the country during World War 2, and 20 years later the Space Program. For France, the high speed rail system (TGV) and the Concorde (viewed as a success early on). For the UK, the National Health Service.

But if you look closely even these examples are deceiving. The victory of the allied forces was only achieved by doubling government spending and throwing every conceivable resource at the war effort. The space program was grossly inefficient, and had to be cut back very significantly once the "showcase" moon landings had been achieved. The French rail system was a success, but again at a very high cost, and currently is being operated in a half-hazard way, with regular strikes, an antiquated website, long lines and poor customer service. The Concorde was scrapped after burning through billions of dollars and ultimately killing hundreds of people.

Compare this track record with the track record of private enterprise which just in the last twenty years brought Google, The iPhone, Amazon, Carbon Nanotubes, Quantum Computing, Uber, Cloud Services and the decoding of the Human Genome. The contest is not even close.

Admittedly, some Asian countries, in particular Singapore and China have shown better results at managing large government projects than the USA or Western Europe. Both countries recruit the very best graduates for careers in government, both tend to pay excellent salaries (greater than private equivalents), and both have organizations that feel closer to well run multinationals to branches of the civil service. The phrase "good enough for government work" is heard in New York, not Singapore or Shanghai. Ronald Reagan's nine most scariest words "I'm from the government and I'm here to help" may not be quite as scary in Chinese.

Planning and Authoritarian Regimes

The examples of planning that do work, as discussed in the previous section, tend to be highly authoritative economies such as Singapore and China. This is not an accident. In his 1942 classic, "The Road To Serfdom", F.A. Hayek has analyzed the connection in great detail, and makes the following points:

-   ultimately planners realize that democracy interferes with their long term plans. "For the benefit of the collective", it is argued that individuals should not interfere with the planning process – ever.

-   The concept of abiding by the "rule of law" is also at odd with pure planning. If who gets what is decided by a central planning group, and who is hired and at what price, then pre-conceived laws need to be thrown out and full authority needs to be given to the state to make whatever decisions it wants

- While state planners may not treat workers as badly as 19th century monopolists, having all decisions controlled by the state effectively is the ultimate monopoly. There is a real loss of freedom here for a perceived (but in many cases not real) sense of economic advantage or equality.

In general, looking back the track record of planned economies is not good. Even Lee Kwan Yu, the father of Singapore, pointed out to Charlie Rose in a recent interview[14] that "Capitalist Systems work better than Planned Ones." The Jury is still out on what China will evolve to in the next 50 years, but it may very well be that it succeeds in becoming the world's largest economy in spite of, and not because, of its authoritarian structure.

Tightly controlled economies such as China do have the advantage of being able to embark on massive infrastructure projects such as high speed rail systems far easier than market economies such as the US. But, as Hayak himself noted in 1942 – "only since everything could be tried – if somebody could be found to back it at their own risk –has science made great strides." Planned economies don't tend to try new things; they decide on a single path of action by consensus and then go down that route in full force.

Trial and error is the key to capitalist innovation. Google wasn't the first search engine, but it used a unique algorithm that hadn't been tested before, and ended up working far better than previous attempts. Now, of course, Google has been copied, like other American technologies in China. But if China is really to lead the world, can they depend on the US to be their R&D lab? And is not conceivable to think that innovation such as Apple, Google and other Silicon Valley "great ideas" may actually increase the lead of the US over other countries in the next 50 years?

Our Economy At A Glance

According to The Bureau of Labor Statistics there were 145 Million Jobs in the United States in 2012, out of a total population of 313 Million people. In other words 42% of the population was actually employed. To put this in context, our demographics break down as follows:

23% -- under 18

63% -- between 18 and 65.

14% -- over 65

If you just look at "employable people" (in the US between 18 and 65, but overall defined as between 15 and 65) – about 67% (or two thirds) of the available labor pool is employed.

Surprisingly, this number is very close (between 65% and 75%) for almost all industrial countries including China. The reason it is not closer to 90% is simply that many women still do not work. Most countries have woman labor participation rates of between 50% and 60%, with China an outlier (just below 70%) and India dead last at 30%.

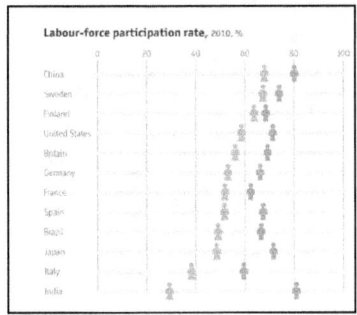

Figure 6 Labor Force Participation Rate, 2010. Source: The Economist

The key fact here is that in two hundred separate countries, with completely separate economies, different demographics, and different ethnic characteristics, the percentage of people who actually work is very constant. *People find jobs.*

This simple fact is ignored by many politicians when they are swayed by fears of job losses due to foreign competition, or when they consider highly inefficient "job creation programs". The simple fact of the matter is that jobs (of some kind) will always materialize.

At the end of the day, it really is not about "creating jobs" – it's about what kind of jobs are being created, and what the overall quality of life is on a per-capita basis. Unemployment rates may make headlines, but, in the aggregate, *employment rates* are steady between 90% and 96%. Generally speaking people in fact *are* working. It's all about what they are doing, and whether their standard of living is going up, down, or staying the same.

Jobs By Sector

At this point, its worthwhile taking a closer look at employment by sector of the economy. It's revealing to see how far we have come to becoming a pure service economy.

Manufacturing	12 million (8%)
Construction	5 million (3%)
State and Local Gov.	19 million (13%)
Federal government	3 million (2%)
Non-gov.t Services	94 million (64%)
Agriculture	2 million (1.5%)
Self employed	9 million (6%)
Total	145 million

Manufacturing now only represents 8% of overall jobs and agriculture less than 2%. The fact of the matter is, it takes fewer and fewer people to make the goods we consume, and the food we eat. Granted, many of the products we consume are now manufactured oversees (in China, for example), but the key fact is that society has massively evolved in the last 100 years from an industrial economy to a close to full employment service one. Karl Marx was wrong in thinking that the middle class would disappear and that there would only be massive amount of workers and a few capitalists. In fact, there are very few industrial workers, period. Technology has replaced workers, and service jobs have emerged to fill the employment void.

Amazingly, 19 million people, or close to 13% of the entire US workforce, is employed by state and local governments. As we will see later, a pattern has emerged where the federal government has shed jobs, but these jobs have re-emerged at the state and local levels. As we will see later on, the headline problems with the US federal deficits are, for many states, far worse on a percentage basis. California, in particular, is a textbook example of out-of-control state government (see *"The Seven Deadly Sins of California Government"* in *The Fourth Revolution* by Micklethwait and Wooldridge).

Other than government, what are these services? Here's a breakdown:

Retail	15 Million (10%)
Wholesale Services	6 Million (5%)
Transportation	4 Million (5%)
Information	3 Million (2%)
Professional and Business	18 Million (12%)
Financial Services	8 Million (6%)
Healthcare	17 Million (12%)
Leisure	14 Million (10%)

These numbers paint a clear picture of the US economy: 20% of us work in logistics and distribution process of goods, from their wholesale distribution, to their transportation and ultimate retail sales. Another 20% work in business services, legal, accounting and financial planning, and information services. And finally another 22% work in healthcare and leisure.

The idea of the 19th century monopolist extracting maximum value from his hordes of underpaid workers is now completely obsolete. At this point, value is created at multiple places on the distribution chain, not solely at the production of "widget" level. Producers of raw, commoditized manufactured goods, such as bulk clothing, automobile parts, children's toys, mass-market watches, and even computers are no longer generating massive returns. Instead, margins for this type of good are being squeezed close to zero, creating downward pressure on prices, not inflation.

Instead, more and more of the economy is becoming service oriented. Great design, computer skills, medical knowledge, management skills, entertainment abilities are being rewarded with higher and higher salaries, while unskilled labor is becoming harder and harder to monetize.

This is where we are now – whether we recognize it or not. Let's now take a step back and see how we got here:

The Evolution of Economic Ideas

In many respects the story of economics can be traced to several "big ideas" that have coalesced over the last four hundred years into deeply held beliefs by the population at large. These ideas are used to re-define history into self-serving myths, which provide a clear narrative to the economic experience.

In their book "The Fourth Revolution"[15] Mickelthwait and Wooldridge divide these ideas into four separate epochs which we can date as follows:

- 1640-1776: The advent of the Nation state, as formulated by Hobbs in *Leviathan*. This is the first notion that the state (at that time ruled by a monarch) has an implicit contract with its citizens to provide them justice and facilitate commerce between them. This is a fundamental departure from earlier forms of royalty where the kind did as he wanted.

- 1777-1900: The growth first of democracy and then of free markets, with Jefferson, Adam Smith and later John Stuart Mill as their advocates. This is an era where government is perceived universally as a bad thing – and the goal of prime ministers such as Gladstone to cut government expenses at all costs (he did). Jefferson's ideal, as expressed in his 1801 inaugural address was "[a] wide and frugal government, which shall restrain men from injuring each other, and leave them otherwise free to regulate their own pursuits of industry and improvement." For America this was a period of (primarily) Republican domination, a period of very small government, no income tax, and completely free immigration.

- 1900-present: The growth of the welfare state, started by the efforts of Beatrice Webb in Britain in the early 1900s, and then added to by FDR, Keynes, Poincare in France, the labor and socialist parties in Britain, and of course the communist revolutions in Russia and China. The authors give a "half revolution" status to the efforts of Thatcher and Reagan to cut government down, but note that those effects have now been broadly reversed. Government is everywhere as big as it has ever been, and is choking the economy.

- 2025+? Mickelthwait posits that we can expect big changes fairly soon, given how close we are to actually running out of money. As he points out the status quo is really the least likely scenario – "when things can't go on, they stop."

The advent of the welfare state has created a myth of the evil robber-baron capitalist in the US and the Dickensian sweatshop in Britain as two horrible things that need stamping out "regardless of cost." However, as Friedman correctly points out, throughout the 1800s there was a steady immigration to the US, despite the sometimes bleak conditions that awaited the immigrants on the other side. It is simply not conceivable that so many people were duped for so long. The reality is that many of them (if not most) found a better life for themselves and their children in the US than abroad.

In the case of the UK, the "big government" welfare ideas of Beatrice Webb and the socialists at the time were again somewhat mythicized for effect. Were there sweatshops? Absolutely. Was the overall standard of living worse than before the industrial revolution? Very debatable. Clearly the intellectuals led towards Marx and Engle's utopian communistic ideals had a conundrum on their hands with Stalin twenty years later.

As the Austrian economist F.A. Hayek described in his book "The Road Towards Serfdom", it was with the best of intentions that these intellectuals were drawn towards the idea of a centrally planned Marxist economy operating under the principal of "from each according to their ability, to each according to their need." Not only they found the same poor economic results discussed earlier, they also found that Socialism in and of itself sowed the seeds for Totalitarianism and Dictatorship. It is no accident that the Nazi party was called the National *Socialist* party. The idea of the command economy, where decisions are made from the top down as opposed to the distributed network defined earlier on here, is core to the very idea of Socialism.

The Evolution of the Welfare State

Beatrice Webb[16], born in London in 1858, was the god-mother of the welfare state we now live under. A British aristocrat with an interest in economics, she grew up reading Karl Marx, and sympathizing with the condition of 19th century British Factory workers. While embracing "collective ownership wherever practicable, collective regulation everywhere else" she formulated her own vision of a socialistic ideal in a ten volume study of local government published between 1906 and 1929.

Webb was highly influential. By campaigning first and foremost for *bigger* government, not a government of the left or the right she initially won friends on all sides. Directly and indirectly this led to free school meals for needy children in 1905, old age pensions in 1906 and national insurance for the sick and unemployed in 1911.

It is worth highlighting that none of these programs existed in any form in the 1800s – in Britain, America or anywhere else. This, in part is what enabled America to have a completely open door immigration policy from 1800 all the way up to 1921. If you don't take have to take care of your immigrants, they are not a burden on your society – only a cheap form of labor. But when you start providing benefits, such as

health, welfare and retirement, even the most left-wing socialists become quite nationalistic. As F.A. Hayak noted, "socialism is for worker's rights – but only for those workers living
inside our national border."

A Recent History of Unexpected Events

Having reviewed the longer term economic history, we will
now turn towards more recent events. Over my lifetime,
which has now spanned four decades, I have seen economy
confound the best and smartest amongst us. Specifically:

- In the 1970s, it seemed like a "sure thing" that we
  would be running out of resources and that commodity prices would be escalating forever. I remember reading "The limits of growth" and thinking that
  my generation would be the last "normal one", before the great apocalypse. I was not alone.

- The exact opposite occurred in the 1980s. Oil prices
  collapsed, and economic activity exploded. Instead of
  "Mad Max Beyond Thunderdome", we got Reagan
  yuppies and tiramisu. The Soviet Union, which
  seemed like a dark, uber-powerful adversary was re-
  vealed as a complete house of cards

- In the late 1980's and early 1990's it seemed that Japan would take over the world. Books like "The Japan that Can Say No[17]", and movies like "Rising
  Sun" portrayed a new economic order – "Made in

Japan." Financial engineering – or "zaibatsu" seemed like an incredibly smart component of the Japanese success story.

- In 1992, the entire Japanese model was unwound. The leverage on the way up caused major problems on the way down; landlords walked away from properties, large banks failed (including ultimately, the Long Term Credit Bank of Japan, the second largest bank in the world at the time).

- In the mid 1990s, when Alan Greenspan first used the term "irrational exuberance" it appeared that we were in some kind of unsustainable bubble that would end imminently. Not only did it keep on going for another 5 years, the Dow Jones doubled and the NASDAQ tripled after his remarks. By 1999, the new tax receipts had created a balanced budget, and one of the smartest investors I have ever met said to me: "Fred, you realize that there never will be another recession again, *ever*".

- Then of course came the "dot com bust", in March 2000, followed by the real estate boom of 2002-2007, fueled (to a large extent) by low interest rates from the Fed and ultra-relaxed lending standards from the leading banks. By 2007, again, very few people were predicting any kind of economic collapse. We again seemed to be marching into a "new world order" –

with the likes of New Century Financial and Washington Mutual as poster children.

-   In 2008-2009, this boom ended followed by the most significant short term bust in living history. It was heavily debated whether we were headed into an inflationary world or a deflationary one. The price of gold spiked from $400 an ounce to $1,400 – seemingly backing the inflationist theories, but real estate went down, and the price of almost everything else stayed about the same.

-   Over the last 5 years, the massive government spending programs across the world have worked on paper : unemployment is way down from the peak, GDP growth is back to normal levels – and most surprisingly – there has been virtually no inflation. People who bought Treasury Inflation Protected Notes (TIPS) have not made money.

The take-away here is that economists have particularly bad records at predicting future changes, or in Warren Buffet's words "they are there to make weathermen look good." Part of this stems, I believe from the flawed idea of treating economics as some kind of "mathematical science." But it is also just a lot of bad thinking following other bad thinking. Just as, in the time of Copernicus, the idea of the earth moving around the sun was viewed as heretical, the idea that controlled economies generally don't work is still being challenged despite the clear evidence of the last 100 years.

Small Events Trigger Big Changes

Another point I am trying to make here is that medium term economic predictions are very difficult. Over just 10 years, the world can – and usually does -- change very dramatically.

In general, the pattern we observe in economics is a slow, steady movement, followed by a very sudden fall. In all cases, this fall is precipitated by seemingly small events.

-   In 1980, Ronald Reagan fired the Air Traffic Controllers, who were on strike and didn't believe they could be fired. This bold move quickly led to the entire demise of American unions, and eventually to the unraveling of wage based inflation pressures.

-   In 1992, a small company scandal -- "The Recruit Company[18]" – triggered the collapse of Japan, Inc.

-   In 2008 an odd form of securities (Collaterized Bond Obligations) brought about the fall of Bear Stearns, a minor Investment Bank. 6 months later, the entire financial system was at risk.

Even Warren Buffet is the first person to admit that he has very little visibility 10 years out. All we can do is use common sense principles to set the fundamental framework for the future: a free market, minimal government intervention, a balanced budget, and a tax structure that does not get in the way of private business.

Free Trade vs. Jobs and Self Sufficiency

While many left-oriented economists still cling to the idea that some form of Socialism might work, there are very few who are left standing fighting free trade.

The arguments against free trade are clear. X Foreign country (replace X with Japan or China depending on the era) is unfairly selling products to us at below cost in order to secure our markets. Inevitably the government of country X is complicit in this, providing to subsidies to the companies manufacturing the product, or "artificially" depressing the $/X exchange rate to make the good "cheaper than it should normally be."

This influx of low cost products is viewed as horribly detrimental to the United States. Never mind the fact that the consumer (who is often a business) is getting these products cheaper than before, and therefor is able to reallocate to other more productive uses – the political fallout is that these imports are costing valuable jobs in the industry that is being targeted.

Now while it is true that the companies in question are right to be fearful, competition is just another fact of life in business. It is not the government's role, for example, to "protect" the paper business form industry from the advent of the paperless office. Nor is its role to "protect" PCs from cheaper tablet computers, whether they are made in the USA or not. Any such interference in the markets only creates false price signals, and can be shown to be – in the aggregate – sub-optimal.

But what about self sufficiency? Surely we cannot depend for all our steel on India or all our oil on the Middle East? Surely we need to defend and nurture our own steel industry and our own oil industry from the standpoint of national security?

Again, this *sounds* appealing, and it does, in point of fact tend to appeal to voters at election time. But the reality is that for any commodity product or service there are always alternatives. Steel can be bought from a number of different countries if any one becomes a problem. The same is true for oil, with the additional caveat that other energy sources, can, over the medium term be substituted for oil if the price of oil rises too much. Already this is happening – the US now derives much of its energy from oil shale, an energy source deemed un-economic just twenty years ago. Price movements and technological advances can dramatically change the status quo.

Wage Controls and The Minimum Wage

Another popular misconception is that raising wages by decree somehow benefits workers. It does not. Whether it is the minimum wage in general, or setting specific union rates for specific classes of work, the impact of wage controls is always the same: it lowers overall employment, reduces profits, and has a negative impact on the economy as a whole.

To quote a Friedman example (updated for today's price levels) if a college kid with low skills can only provide a useful service at $6 an hour, and if the minimum wage is $10 – the college kid will not be offered a job). This does not benefit the kid (he is not working), nor does it benefit society as a whole, which would save $4 per hour by substituting the kid's labor for some higher priced labor. The only person benefiting in the equation is the person already employed who does not face the labor competition from the college kid.

It is no wonder then that minimum wage laws are most heavily advocated by big labor unions, whose members make substantially more than the minimum wage – and not by the people who you might expect would benefit – the unemployed.

Rules, Rules and More Rules

One of the characteristics of an economy dominated by Olson's law is that special interests tend to erect barriers at federal, state and local levels to prevent competition in all things. In Chapter 2 of his book "Free to Choose" Milton Friedman enumerates a few of these: rules exist to prevent people from raising money in capital markets, from operating a taxicab, from working overtime in many instances or from selling electricity to your neighbor. Adds Mickelthwait in "The Fourth Revolution":

> "If you want to work in the wig trade in Texas you
> need to take 300 hours of classes and pass an exam.

Alabama obliges manicurists to sit through 750 hours of instruction. Florida will not let you work as an interior designer unless you complete a four year university degree and a two-year apprenticeship and pass a two hour exam."

These rules in aggregate are creating a Kafka-esque bureaucracy where you need some kind of permit do make money doing anything. They are not in the best interest of the economy. What they are in the interest of is congressmen who can use them to buy votes from special interest groups.

How can we combat the increasing proliferation of this type of state and federal law? One possibility, suggested by Micklethwait and Wooldridge is to have sunset periods for every new law. If laws required re-instating every 4 or 8 years, there would not be as many of them. Another possibility, suggested by friend Jim Willenborg, is to have a cap on the absolute number of laws. Want to add a new piece of legislation? Find some older piece of legislation to remove. In practice this might be extremely hard to do – not necessarily a bad thing. Finally, we could subject every piece of legislation to an online referendum. If a certain threshold of votes was made against an existing law, then that law might need to be reconfirmed by some voting process after a set period of time.

The point here is that legislation itself in now out of control. Recognizing that it has become a problem is the first step towards finding a solution. A number of approaches can and should be tried to cut back on the absolute number of laws.

The Information Economy

As we have seen, the vast majority of jobs are now firmly in the service sector, as opposed to manufacturing and farms. But within the service sector itself, information is becoming the new currency, the new "wealth of nations." Apple Computer is not so much a computer manufacturing company as a design company, a human user interface company. Amazon is not a "commerce" company as it is a logistics company that is harnessing the power of the internet to completely redefine the distribution of goods.

In some sense, "information" isn't new. Certainly the steel mill and even the steam engine were discoveries based of "information" and "technology." The difference now is Information itself is completely separate from the use of the Information. At the extreme a company like Rambus[19] does not design products at all; it designs key patents that are broadly used in (electronic) products. With the Internet, there is a complete separation (and sharing) of our intellectual DNA, and the "protein factories" that take this code and turn it into "flash and blood."

Countries that are still protecting commodity industries such as steel or even automobiles are missing the key point. The main resource of the 21rst century is ideas, intellectual capital, and not plant and equipment, factory assembly lines and the production of mass market widgets.

Here, juggernauts such as China, Russia and Brazil are at a distinct disadvantage relative to the US. Yes, they can embark on massive infrastructure projects, but can they innovate? Can they try hundreds or even thousands of ideas before they find the good ones? Given the type of innovation that we can perceive lies ahead (nanotechnology, atomic fusion, genetic engineering, robotics), it seems like a good bet that the smartest nation, not necessarily the one with the most people, or even the most engineers, will win. In this regard the US is still very well positioned for the 21rst century.

Economics Simplified – Summary

There are not very many areas of human research that can be summed up in a few paragraphs. Economics however, does fall into that category. Essentially Adam Smith had it right in 1776 – the optimal way to organize an economy is to let the free market decide. Free trade in all cases trumps imports. Wage controls, tariffs, rules and excessive regulations in almost cases limit growth and hurt the economy as a whole.

Socialism, communism, and the development of the modern welfare state have all failed to deliver on their promises. The ideas behind them were and still are well meaning. Unfortunately, they just don't work. Central planning lacks the kind of price signals and internal incentives to create the kind of products a modern world needs efficiently. Welfare states discourage work and the establishment of new business and technology. Still, as Mancur Olson observes, rot can set in even in purely free market economy, with specialized interests colluding to limit overall growth. Free Markets are a necessary, but not sufficient condition for prosperity.

6. A Simple Flat Tax

ONE OF THE MOST IMPORTANT ASPECTS of any government is how big it should be, and how it should be funded.

In order to answer these questions, we need to take a look at historical data, and put things back on a common perspective. Historically, the federal government spends very close to 20% of GDP, as graph below illustrates.

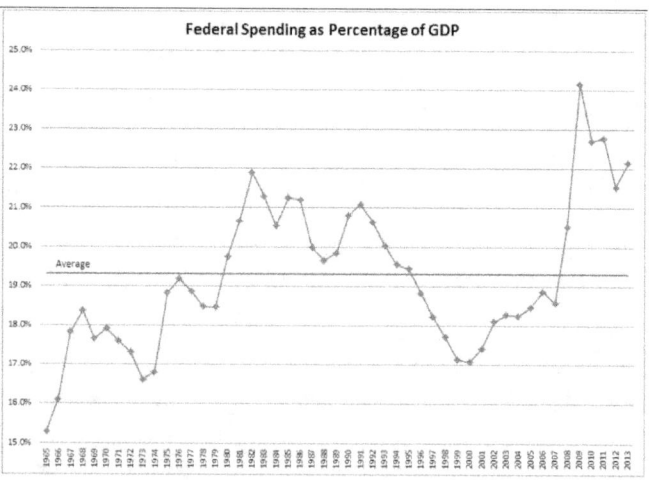

Amazingly, whether the administration is democrat or republican, this number has been trapped in the 17% to 24% for the last 50 years. Even with a 70% marginal tax rate it stayed at 20% -- people just stopped earning or delayed cap gains or hired more accountants or tax lawyers. Note that this does not mean that it is the right number, but it does mean that any significant deviation from 20% will be very hard to accomplish.

Now in the US, unlike other countries, the federal government is only responsible for half the overall spending. The other half is split evenly between state and local spending. Taken altogether, the US Total Spending bill is about 41.6% (source: the 2014 Index of Economic Freedom by the Heritage Foundation and The Wall Street Journal). This is almost identical with Brazil (39%) and Japan (42%), and quite a bit lower than Germany (45%), the United Kingdom (48.5%) and France (56.1%).

Focusing back again strictly on the federal government, the 20% number seems generally *reasonable overall.* Could it be 10%? Could both state and federal government be *half* current levels? China's are – they are running at 23% of GDP in overall spend; Singapore is running at just 17%. So it is possible – but probably not an achievable goal for the United States. And probably not desirable either; let's not forget that the United States is the most successful economy in the world, so the mix of government spending over the last 50 years is probably not *vastly off* optimal levels.

Let's put aside for the time being the question of where the federal money is being spent, and look strictly at how it should be raised. Traditionally this comes from four main sources:

- Individual Income Taxes (47%)
- Social Security Taxes (34%)
- Corporate Taxes (10%)
- Excise and Other Taxes (9%)

The Bulk of Receipts come from individuals, not corporations. Between income taxes and Social Security taxes, this represents 81% of every dollar coming in.

As I will argue later on, Social Security as a "product" needs to be killed. It's confusing the accounting of the deficit, it's not self sustainable, and its ultimate raison d'etre – providing retirement benefits to less fortunate workers can easily be subsumed in the overall mission of the federal budget. The simple approach calls for taxing individuals once, not twice.

Individual Taxes

As mentioned above, it is individuals, not corporations who pay taxes, and that is the way it should be. But how can we simplify individual taxes? The answer is to eliminate Social Security, and combine both in a single flat tax.

In 2013, Total Tax Receipts were 2.7 trillion dollars. Total Personal Income stood at 13 trillion dollars. Dividing, we can see that a 20 % flat tax rate would just about cover the entire thing.

$$13 \text{ Trillion} \quad x \quad 20\% \quad = 2.6 \text{ Trillion}$$

(income)   tax rate   taxes

The benefit of a simple, clean flat tax rate like this far exceed the simple collection of revenues.

- Exactly 20% would be withheld from every paycheck. No need for withholdings or anything else.

- Dramatically simplifies tax collection. There are no more deductions, tiers or alternative minimum taxes. Just enter how much you make. Multiply by 20%. That is the total tax owed.

- Harder to game. Right now, smaller incremental taxes are added every year in efforts to boost revenue. This adds to the overall complexity of the system, and goes against transparency. With a flat 20% tax, it will be clear if the government is overspending

- More predictable. Right now, the Office of Management of the Budget employs thousands of people whose job is to predict what revenues might look like 5, 10 or more years in the future. Because of the complexity of the tax code, this is like looking into tea leaves. A simple flat tax would dramatically help.

There should be no difference between capital gains and ordinary income. Regardless of how you make your money – you owe the government a flat 20%. Day trade a share of GOOG? Pay 20% on your profits. Make $100,000 a year as a consultant? Pay 20%. Make $30,000 as a factory worker? Pay 20%.

No Deductions

One of the reasons that our tax code is so complex is the infamous principal of section 62 of our tax code that states that any expense involved in the production of income can be written off. Each of these "deductions" from your top line income has its own rules. They include

- Accounting and Legal Fees
- Charitable Donations
- Medical Expenses
- Mortgage Interest
- Parking and Tolls
- Losses due to Theft
- Credit Card Fees

Each of these "exceptions" was created for a specific reason, but over time evolved to suit completely separate interests. The mortgage interest deduction, for example was originally created for small businesses, not homeowners, since, as the Center for Federal Tax Policy correctly points out:

> "Congress could not have had homeownership in mind. The great majority of people who owned a home did not have a mortgage. The exceptions were farmers. But most folks bought their homes with cash; they had no mortgage interest to deduct."

The mortgage deduction represents Olson's law in its purest form. According to the US Census bureau, there are 75 million homeowners in the United States. Since 1950, the widest margin of victory in a popular election was 18 million votes (Nixon over McGovern, 1972). So this special interest of affluent Americans represents *a full three times* the amount of votes needed to win the presidency.

Adds Mark Calabria of the Cato organization points out[20], this deduction distorts home prices upwards, causing the average homeowner family to get far more into debt than they otherwise should. It doesn't actually tend to increase home ownership, since it is mainly used by upper middle class tax payers who would almost certainly still buy a house if the deduction did not exist. In effect, it is simply a transfer of money from the younger first time homeowners to the older, richer retirees.

The Bottom Third.

Opponents of the flat tax often argue that it is not "progressive", that lower income families deserve to "pay less" while the rich should be taxed at a higher rate. These are, in essence two separate arguments; on one hand there is the question of what the bottom third should be paying in taxes (assuming they pay anything), on the other hand, there is question of how we should tax the affluent class.

Currently, less than half of Americans pay any kind of tax at all. So while the argument is pitched as upper class versus lower class, it really is about the taxation of various strata of the middle class. Given that we are in favor of taxable cash welfare payments to the bottom third, the effective tax rate is in fact progressive, up until we pass the welfare limit.

For people who are not receiving welfare, the argument against a uniform flat tax is less convincing. Is it really philosophically wrong that a family making $50,000 a year pay $10,000 in taxes while another family making $100,000 a year pay $20,000 ? The numbers not only seem to make sense, they seem, in fact, fair. And, if we eliminate all forms of deductions, getting 20% of everything Bill Gates and Warren Buffet make is also a fair deal for society. Certainly, we could charge them more, but there are very few of them, and the simple round figure should be more than sufficient to pay for everything the government does.

As we will discuss later, there is a strong case to be made that welfare and other payments should be taxable, and additive to temporary or part time work. This is a critical component of incentivizing people to get off welfare and get back to regular employment. Welfare payments should just be viewed as another source of funds that only very low income people are entitled to. And those people should pay 20%, just like everybody else.

Paying Your Taxes Online

One of the big advantages of a dramatically simplified tax code is that it tax collection and payment could all be easily be done online, at the US government portal. In particular, all wages could be reported directly to that portal, and you could add / correct these easily:

Name: Joe Smith

Tax Year: 2015

Wages: ACME Corp:	$45,000	(edit)
Consulting:	$ 5,000	(edit)
+ add new		
Total Wages	$50,000	
Taxes: 20%	$10,000	
Withholdings	-$9,000	

Taxes Due:	$1,000	

The balance could be paid using any number of credit cards, PayPal, Bitcoin or other payment mechanisms, or by direct payment from e-cash (see the next chapter). Right now, due to the massive complexity in the tax code, this is just not possible to do this for 90% of Americans.

Corporate Taxes

Corporate Taxes are only a small fraction of overall taxes. Its politically easy to attack corporations for *not paying their fair share* – especially as they don't vote. In reality this is single worst place to look for tax revenue. The fact is that companies create jobs, and by taxing companies, as well as the people who own shares in them, you are only reducing the competitiveness of America as a hub for global capital.

Many countries are using low corporate tax rates to encourage companies to establish presences there. In many cases the headline tax rate needs to adjusted for other taxes to get an effective blended rate. The following data is from Forbes:

Bahamas:	12%
Bermuda:	12%
Ireland:	12.5%
Cayman Islands:	13%
Malaysia:	17%
India:	17%
Taiwan:	18%
Sweden:	18%
Switzerland:	18%

Canada:	21%
China:	22%
USA:	28% (excludes state tax)
Japan:	38%

Effective Corporate Tax Rates, 2013 (Source: Forbes)

As a director of a (small) multi-national corporation, I can assure you that these numbers matter. Why, all other things equal, would I set up shop in the USA or Japan and pay three times the tax as in Ireland? The answer is: I wouldn't. It may be difficult to operate a manufacturing or other people inten-sive industry in the Bahamas, but Ireland is certainly a viable possibility for many types of businesses; the labor force is educated, cost effective and draws from the entire EU (so it scales). Similarly, if the cost of doing business in the US was reduced, one could definitely see large multinationals moving to the US for cost reasons. Right now we are just not com-petitive.

The "simple" solution to this is just reduce corporate tax rates to zero and keep them there.

- Foreign companies would immediately move to the United States, creating millions of new jobs, and driving up our labor costs. We would be the absolute best place worldwide to start a company.

- American companies would stay in the US instead of relocating to places such as Ireland, or even (on paper) to the Cayman Islands.

- Companies would become more far more profitable, and would use those extra profits to grow, by hiring and by investing in technology and capital equipment

I realize that this "simplification" is political dynamite. It seems outrageous that a company like Exxon Mobil (or even Apple) would make billions of dollars in profit and not pay a penny in tax, when hard working middle class families struggle to make ends meet. As Yoda said in Star Wars: "Simple yes. Easy no." This is a case where the right decision is taking a bitter pill. It looks and tastes awful, but it's the right thing to do.

We want more multinationals in the USA, not less. We want more companies hiring workers, bidding up wages, building new plant and equipment and new infrastructure in *our* country. We shouldn't *complain* about tax cheats, we should *compete*. And don't forget that if there are any people who are good at avoiding paying taxes, its large corporations. We can try taxing them all we want, even if they stay in the US, large companies will avoid paying taxes. Or, if we push them to the limit, as they have done in several socialist economies, they will simply go bankrupt.

The one area that does need to be addressed is the potential use of this structure by rich individuals. It is relatively easy for anybody in the top 5% to set up a corporation to put personal assets in. If that corporation is not a pass through, and has a 0% tax rates, then any asset bought or sold in that corporation would not generate revenue for the government – at least until it was distributed back to the beneficiary.

This sounds again, tremendously unfair, but in reality isn't. Suppose Scrooge McDuck moves his entire fortune into Duck Inc. He then buys shares in other companies, sells them and builds up a huge positive balance in Duck Inc. Any time the money is actually distributed back to Scrooge McDuck, it then becomes taxable. If Scrooge is a good investor, then the government will benefit from his compound rate of return, whether he is buying US assets or indeed foreign shares. If he is not, then there wouldn't have been profits or taxes in the first place.

Dividends

The "Simplify" rule applies to corporate dividends as well. It's tempting to try to find revenue at any all points in the economic process, and erecting a toll bridge at the profit off-ramp of corporations might seem a reasonable place to go looking. It's not.

Taxing dividends in the end does not result in more tax overall tax revenues. All you are doing is taxing the same economic event three times: once at the corporate level, once at the dividend level, and once at the individual level.

All you are doing by taxing dividends is to encourage companies not to pay them, and encourage investors not to invest in those companies. Investors can overlook the fact that a growth company such as Google does not pay a dividend; but for a more mature company like Exxon Mobil, Investors amazingly are insistent that they get a return of capital as well as a return on it.

The Cato Institute, generally a voice of reason on these matters, has this to add:

> "First, high dividend taxes add to the income tax code's general bias against savings and investment. Second, high dividend taxes cause corporations to rely too much on debt rather than equity financing. Highly indebted firms are more vulnerable to bankruptcy in economic downturns. Third, high dividend taxes reduce the incentive to pay out dividends in favor of retained earnings. That may cause corporate executives to invest in wasteful or unprofitable projects."

Simple is good. Zero corporate taxes and zero dividends across the board would be a huge dramatic boom to the economy. With the US infrastructure and our (current) pole position in the world economy, we would quickly re-emerge as the country to beat.

Excise taxes.

Excise taxes are taxes on specific goods, such as gasoline and tobacco. The idea is not new – As early as 1776, Adam Smith wrote:

> "It has for some time past been the policy of Great Britain to discourage the consumption of spirituous liquors, on account of their supposed tendency to ruin the health and to corrupt the morals of the common people."

In many countries, such as Australia and Singapore, large gas guzzling cars like Range Rovers are subject to additional taxes of 100% or more. My personal experience traveling to those countries indicates that people don't seem to mind this "luxury" tax. In a perverse way, it makes the items even more desirable and unique, while limiting their overall absolute numbers.

In general, I am in favor of excise taxes in a limited way more to incentivize social change than as a tool for revenue collection. Smoking, gas-guzzling automobiles, gambling, and alcohol consumption should be discouraged. This, in conjunction with incentives for health and education could bring positive benefits to our nation.

The Hidden Costs of Complicated Taxes.

In a recent article in Foreign Affairs, Steven Teles[21] notes that the sheer size of the tax system is a huge burden to society.

> "The transaction costs of the tax code are just as impressive and disturbing. The American tax code is almost certainly the most complicated in the Western world. The Internal Revenue Service's taxpayer advocate estimates that in 2008 the direct and indirect costs of complying with that complexity amount to $163 billion each year. Included in that cost are the remarkable 6.1 billion hours a year that American individuals and businesses spend complying with the filing requirements of the tax code."

The IRS estimates are in fact probably low. The fact that all this time and money is spent on just preparing taxes does not capture the reverse benefits of a clear, predictable system. If businesses and individuals can clearly understand how the state is taxing them, they can plan accordingly, and make better decisions. Time and time again, history has shown us that simplifying systems in this fashion has tremendous long term advantages.

A Simple Flat Tax – Summary.

This chapter is an attempt to make the case for a much simpler tax system, with a single 20% flat individual tax, no social security tax, no corporate taxes, no dividend tax, and no distinction between capital gains and ordinary income. Workers will understand what is going out of their paychecks much more easily, tax preparation will not be the nightmare that it currently is, and the government will be able to plan its revenues much better.

7. A Simple Balanced Budget

SO FAR WE HAVE GIVEN SOME GENERAL ARGU-
MENTS IN FAVOR OF SIMPLICITY, we have outlined
the technical infrastructure for government in the 20th century, and we have suggested a radical, flat tax simplification to
the way the state *collects revenues*. We now turn to the general
problem of our balance sheet.

This problem has two key components. First of all, our overall federal and state *debt* levels have now hit critical levels
where business as usual is no longer an option. The second is
that in the face of this, our federal and state *deficits* are still
completely out-of-control, and show very little long term
signs of improving.

For a government such as the US to experience short term
periods of high government deficits is not a problem – as
long as these deficits are isolated, and rectified by subsequent
surpluses or even long periods of balanced budgets. But on
the federal and state level this is not what is happening; we
have used up our lifelines and are heading straight towards a
brick wall. We will hit it within a generation.

As we will show, the problem is costs. For decades now, growth in federal government spending has greatly exceeded the growth in the overall economy, and also consistently exceeded the growth in taxation. Over the years these percentages have added up to create a debt level that is now only addressable in the best of cases by decades of cost control. The state deficit problem is more recent, but the severity of the problem is in many cases worse than the federal one.

The only viable solution to these problems are balanced budgets – which at this point can only be accomplished by massive spending cuts. "Revenue enhancement" is just not an option – raising taxes for example may very well lower the actual amount of tax revenues collected; it certainly cannot, from these levels, solve the problem.

It will be painful. As New Jersey Governor Chris Chrissie said, "the only choices we have left are the choices that people have said were politically impossible. It's not an income problem, it's a benefit problem. We have to cut benefits" (source: 60 minutes, 2010).

Painful, but (no longer) impossible. *All* we need to do is cut out bloated federal and state programs by 30%, more or less across the board. Chrissie did it in New Jersey. California needs to follow his example, and so does the federal government. Millions will be affected, but, to put things in perspective, the pain impact will be far less than a major war.

If we don't do it, insolvency or hyperinflation await. We can go the way of Argentina, and just renounce our debt, or the way of Zimbabwe and add multiple zeros to every banknote. Either alternative comes with massive unemployment and complete financial wipeout for vast sectors of the population. The choice is ours.

Government Debt around the World

How bad is the problem? Despite hearing about our debt and deficits constantly, very few among us have a good grasp at the numbers.

The correct way to think about government debt is relative to (nominal) GDP. The higher that ratio – the more unstable the situation is.

The following table shows this ratio for the major industrialized nations. We've also added Singapore for reference, just to point out that Singapore is far from perfect as an economic model.

Japan	214%
Singapore	112%
USA	106%
UK	90%
France	90%
Canada	84%
Germany	80%
Brazil	54%

Switzerland	52%
India	49%
China	31%
Russia	12%

Debt to GDP ratios 2014, by country.

The Lessons From Japan

The first thing that stands out with this data is Japan. In 1990, the Japanese stock market collapsed and Japan embarked on a massive deficit spending program that is very similar to our post 2009 "Tarp" bill.

Japan built roads, bridges, and massive excess infrastructure that, in the words of one observer "turned the entire country into one giant parking lot." At the same time, the government forced interest rates down to zero – in a move that completely foreshadowed Ben Bernanke's policy at the Federal Reserve.

The numbers are now in and the results are abysmal. The Japanese stock market is still one third of the peak level of 1990 (almost a quarter decade ago). Japanese unemployment is at record highs. The Chinese economy, which was less than a third of the Japanese economy in 1990 is now larger.

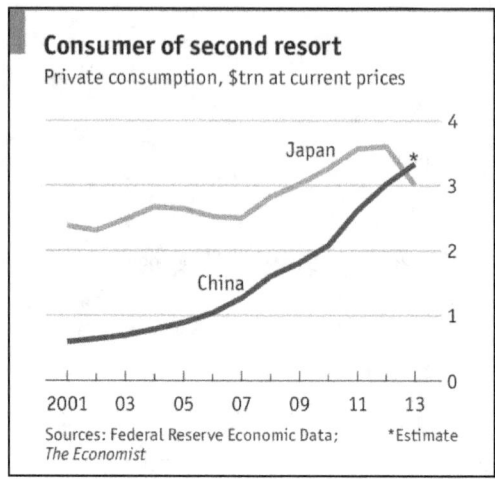

Consumer of second resort
Private consumption, $trn at current prices

Japan

China

2001 03 05 07 09 11 13

Sources: Federal Reserve Economic Data; *Estimate
The Economist

Clearly, large keysian deficit programs just don't work as a long term plan. They might have worked in the very short term under FDR, but the idea of using asphalt as a key driver of economic progress in 21rst century is lunacy.

Common sense tells us that building bridges to nowhere and putting people to work on massive public work projects is not productive. Developing state of the art technology, and advanced manufacturing processes is. And that is not something any government, ever, has shown any capability of doing. Keynes, and his 21rst century counterpart, Paul Krugman, need to be seriously discredited.

Going back to Japan, we note that at 200% the debt to GDP ratio is un-fundable at anything other than close to zero interest rates. Funding 200% of GDP at, say, 5%, would cost 10%

of GDP. But taxes collected in modern economies max out at 20% of GDP – so at 5%, a country like Japan would be spending half of its entire budget on interest.

It should be noted that Governments ultimately set the interest rates that they pay on their own debt. In the case of Japan, there are significant internal pools of savings that are being used, at next to zero interest rates, to fund this massive deficit. In the case of the US, this is not the case, as out debt is held, to a great degree, by foreign countries such as China and Russia. These countries could easily choose not to buy any longer term US government bonds, in which case the government would have to borrow entirely short term – in effect printing money (and loaning it to the banks).

The Growth of Government Spending

Over the last 50 years, in terms of number of employees, the federal government has remained relatively constant. 2.7 Million people worked for the executive branch of the government in 1966, and 2.7 Million people work there today. Over the same period, the military has shrunk from 3.1 Million people to 1.5 Million today. This would appear to be going in the right direction, and makes sense considering the improvements in technology over the last 50 years. Parkinson's law would seem to have been thwarted at the federal level.

What is alarming, however is the fact that even without more people, government spending levels as a percentage of GDP have risen to beyond the peak of WW2 spending.

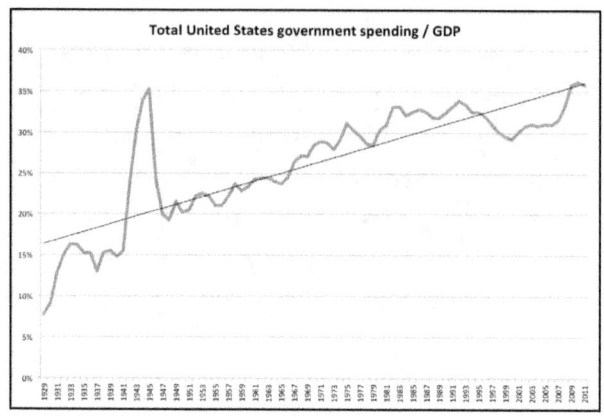

Total government Spending Relative To GDP. Hello WW2!

As the above chart shows, government spending represented 35% of the entire economy in 2011 – more than during the peak years of World War 2. And if 35% is the direct spend, the secondary effects are north of 50%. Today, almost half the voters now will clearly suffer if government is in any way curtailed. Asking these people to vote against their immediate self interest is now extremely difficult.

Going back to 1900, the situation is almost unrecognizable. There was no federal income tax, no federal reserve and very modest debt loads relative to GDP. Immigration was completely free and open – with the US population increasing from 7 million in 1800 to 70 million by 1900. The US was already an extremely evolved economy, well on its way to becoming the world's largest.

To use a Republican line, the last century truly has been a century of "tax and spend" – a significant part of it, of course, under Republican leadership. We are now at a point where this straight line up and to the right must, of necessity bend or fall. There is no place upwards to go.

Other Countries Spend / GDP

The key number to hold on to from the previous section is 35% -- that's how much money our government is spending relative to our overall economy. We have seen where that is historically – at a new all time high, and equal to the peak spending levels of World War II. But how is it compared to the rest of the world?

The Heritage Foundation provides the data[22]:

> France 56%
> Sweden 51%
> UK 48%
> Germany 45%
> Japan 42%
> US 42%
> Australia 35%
> Singapore 17%

Growth in Outsourcing and Entitlements

It's important to re-iterate, that in a remarkable twist on Parkinson's law, the government is now getting bigger *without* adding headcount. It is doing so in two fundamental ways:

- By indirectly allocating resources to private companies such as pharmaceutical companies, medical insurance companies and defense contractors.

- By increasing benefits and entitlements one special interest group at a time – with the effect that nearly everybody in some way benefits from government re-distribution.

Let's take a deeper look at the first point. Starting with Reagan the Defense department has become largely outsourced to outside contractors. This trend, which was continued under Bush 1, Clinton, Bush 2 and Obama, has been hugely beneficial to the stocks of Defense companies.

Figure 7 Shares of Boeing Aircraft

In 1982, Boeing Aircraft was at a split adjusted $3 a share. In 2014, 32 years later, the price is 132, a return, (excluding dividends!) of 40x. In contrast the Dow Jones itself was about 1,000 at the time, and would have provided a much more modest gain of 16x.

The amount of federal spending contracts is now epic. The following table shows the largest 7 beneficiaries – and they are all defense companies:

Lockheed Martin	$36 Billion
Boeing	$19 Billion
Northrop Grumman:	$17 Billion
General Dynamics:	$15 Billion
Raytheon:	$15 Billion
United Technologies:	$7 Billion
L3 Communications:	$7 Billion

	$116 Billion

Largest federal Beneficiaries: Source Top 100 Contractors Report, US
government.

To put this number in perspective, total individual income
taxes in 2014 were 1,386 Billion. So 8 cents of every tax dollar
you pay goes to one of these 7 defense firms!

Defense contracting represents a very visible aspect of out-
sourcing. But an equally large, if much less visible phenomenon is the indirect allocation of resources to the insurance
and pharmaceutical sector. As we will discuss at length in
Chapter 11, healthcare is now the single largest line item in
the budget. The share prices of large insurance companies,
the main beneficiaries of this splurge, mirror those of Defense contractors.

But the real growth is in entitlements. Between welfare and
healthcare benefits, entitlements are now north of a trillion
dollars a year – and that does not include social security. We
will go into this subject in greater detail later, but we wanted
to flag the raw numbers first.

Once again, the government has outsourced its "solution" to
the healthcare problem to a complex web of interested parties. Insurance companies and Big Pharma clearly have an
interest in the status quo. Not surprisingly, some of these
Insurance companies have been amazing long term stocks to
own.

Humana – the largest healthcare insurance company. The stock has gone from 5 in 2000 to 124 in 2014. – a gain of over 20x.

Any attempt to fix government needs to address healthcare. It's simply too big of an issue, and growing too rapidly to be ignored. The elephant in the room, as I mentioned is obesity: we are all, as a species, eating too much and becoming un-healthy.

State Balance Sheets

Although the federal Deficit budget problems are front and center, the state budgets are in many cases, in similarly bad shape. They are simply not as newsworthy because each problem is somewhat different, but as 60 Minutes highlighted in 2010, the problem is perhaps the single biggest threat to the US Economy.

Overall, state Debt levels relative to state GDP range from 4% (Wyoming) to 27% (New York), with an average of 17%. These numbers are significantly lower than the equivalent federal ratios – but bear in mind that the tax rates are also significantly lower. The national state average tax burden is 9.9% according to the tax institute, versus about double (about 18%) for the federal government. So relative to taxes collected, the overall indebtedness of the state of NY is approaching federal levels.

And debt is only part of the problem. The bigger problem is the massive amount of unfunded state pension liabilities. Remember that unlike the federal government, which hasn't grown much in headcount over the last fifty years, the state and local governments represent 13% of all jobs in the nation. Here, the problem is not only financial mismanagement, but simply demographics: there are a lot more people to support than ever thought possible.

Here the issue is not so much taking away jobs or benefits that people enjoy today, it is awakening them to the sad reality that their futures will almost certainly be more difficult than they had previously thought. As Chrissie explained to Sixty Minutes "I simply don't have the money in my budget. Simple as that."

Again, the problem is psychologically and politically difficult, but not insurmountable. Just as with unfunded federal liabilities, the solution can be as simple as raising the retirement age

– a proposal passed into law by California Governor Jerry Brown in 2012.

A Balanced Budget Amendment

Turning back to the federal deficit, the problem, to re-iterate, is out of control government spending. To solve this problem, we now need to get this spending back under control which means balancing the budget, quickly, decisively, and permanently.

Ronald Reagan fought for, and never got, a balanced budget amendment. 20 years later, under George Bush, Dick Cheney famously said "deficits don't matter". We now have a situation where, if interest rates returned to "normal" levels, every penny of individual income taxes would have to go to just paying interest on the debt.

The problem here is one of discipline. Our political system has none. Like a teenager with a messy room, the room will always be cleaned "tomorrow". Except, of course, it never will. Unless we draw a line in the sand and insist that the budget be balanced, it will never be.

Like many other people, I used to believe that the idea of a balanced budget amendment was "simplistic". Of course, *it is*. It's a simple – good – idea, that our government needs to control its spending, and not spend more than it brings in every year. Any family or business knows that this is the only way you can survive for anything more than a very short amount of time. In the case of the US government, our time is close to being up.

Its easy to justify "a little overspending." Most corporations use debt as well as equity in the capital structure; why shouldn't the government? Can't we reasonably afford to keep a debt that is close to one years worth of GDP? We've always had debt – why stop now?

These are all reasonably good questions, which might make sense if the debt levels were not so elevated, and if the government showed any kind of ability to revert back to a surplus in time. We are beyond that point. At this stage, we need to either get the budget under control, or we could very well face insolvency in the next 20 years. And all of this because we are consistently spending 30% more than we are taking in.

In this chapter we will argue that a simple, balanced budget must be the absolute cornerstone of a good 21th century government. Those governments that do balance their budgets and keep their debt under control will survive. Those that don't will eventually fail. And eventually could very well be within the lifetime of the reader, and could very well include the United States of America.

An Idealized Budget

So what can we do? How should we approach the budget and actually balance it – at least conceptually, from the top down?

Our overall solution is to budget both taxes and spending as a percentage of revenue. As we saw in the previous chapter, we argued for a flat 20% federal tax rate. This is roughly the amount of money we currently take in, and should be a reasonable initial target for the size of the federal budget.

Starting at this level, here is how we now see the budget:

Tax Receipts:	20% of Income
Defense	about 5%
Medical + Welfare	about 5%
Social Security	about 5%
Everything Else	about 5%

Sounds simplistic? Good. It should. Anything more complex than this is bound to fail. Note that the amounts are set as a percentage of Total Aggregate Taxable Income, which increases proportionally to nominal GDP. In other words, this budget is completely *scalable*.

Note that I have used the word "about 5%" to discuss each of the four key spending areas. It's very possible that one might be 4% and another 6%. The key is that a balanced budget is in fact completely achievable. It might be painful for 2-4 years, but ultimately the economy will adjust.

Waiting it Out

On the positive side, GDP is growing at 3% annually on a real rate, and about 6% on a nominal rate. With respect to the budget, it's the nominal rate that is important – as that is the rate that applies to taxable income. What this means is that in a little over 10 years the economy will double in nominal terms, over 20 years quadruple. *If* we can hold the current system in place for that long (a big *if*) – we can overcome the budgetary problems we currently face.

Regardless of whether the US economy "muddles through" or not, the current system is far from ideal. It's also far from inevitable. Other countries, in particular, Singapore, Hong Kong and Switzerland have far stronger underlying financial underpinnings. We should follow their example.

Now I am sure some readers will stop me here by saying that these countries are "different" or "smaller" and that somehow their experience "does not apply". To this I answer that all countries are different. The fact the United States is the largest economy on the planet does not give it an excuse to be poorly run. In fact, if it continues to be run in this fashion, it very well may not be the largest economy in the near future. History has a way of not caring

Government Pay

One way to balance the budget involves the pay levels of government employees. As the Cato Institute points out in its report *"How to Spend 3.9 Trillion"*[23], it is egregious.

"In 2012 average wages and benefits for federal civilian workers were \$114,976, or 74 percent more than the average for U.S. private-sector workers of \$65,917. Federal benefits are particularly out of line with the private sector. A good place to save taxpayer money would be to scale back federal pension benefits."

The Risk of Hyper-Inflation

One of the cornerstones of a solid economy is a solid currency. What we don't want is the experience of Argentina, Brazil, or, Zimbabwe.

A Hundred Billion Zimbabwe Dollars. Could it happen here?

All three of these economies – in the last 50 years – went through periods of hyper-inflation. All three started with (reasonably) stable, modern economies. In all three cases, all prior cash was rendered close to worthless, and the economy had (has to in the case of Zimbabwe) to be restarted from scratch.

How realistic a risk is this? It's definitely *possible*, considering that in 2009 the government came very close to a complete financial wipeout. Some would argue that it is even *probable*, given the size of our government debt. At some point, unless things change, the interest alone on our debt could exceed taxable income. In that scenario, every penny of taxes goes to pay our debtors, with the debt itself exploding exponentially until the entire system collapses.

Are we close to this point? Yes – and no. Currently, the system is barely sustainable; but only because interest rates are held (by the Federal Reserve) close to zero. At an average long term historical interest rate of, say 5%, the interest alone on our debt would be a trillion dollars – about the equivalent of all personal income tax receipts. So we are definitely close to the "flash point" – but not there yet.

Actually Balancing The Budget

Politically, things are very hard until they become very easy. A trillion dollar deficit seemed the absolute maximum that our economy could support until the crash of 2009. At that point, the government OK'd a 2 trillion dollar deficit in order to save off a second great depression. Going back further, in World War 2, the entire country mobilized with a single goal – to fight Germany and Japan. Money was literally printed to fund the war.

Could the same sense of urgency apply in reverse to creating a stable, sound government with a balanced budget and a long-term viable currency? I believe it could. The only question is whether this will be before or after a massive economic depression. Because its pretty clear to me that unchecked, this is likely where we are heading.

So let's assume for a moment that cooler heads prevail and that one way or another a new administration is elected with a mandate to sanity to the system. What would that administration do?

First, as mentioned, it would reduce all major forms of expenditures down by 30%, effective immediately. For the sake of clarity, let's spell this out

Defense spending	-30%
Retirement Benefits	-30%
Medical benefits	-30%
All other programs	-30%

This sounds painful, and it is. But is no more or less painful than a company cutting its expenses by a third, or a family downsizing. This happens all the time, to all of us, in different circumstances. Is it painful? Yes. Is it the end of the world? No.

Since government is currently about 20% of GDP, a reduction of 30% in the overall size of the government would reduce GDP by about 6% for a single year. But, remember, that GDP grows on a nominal level by about 6% per year, so all this means, is that on a nominal level would not change much during the year of the "big cut". And, it would be a one time event. After that, we would have a government with

- a balanced budget
- a stronger currency
- a simple 20% flat tax
- much better long term viability

A Simple Balanced Budget – Summary.

A great product must be sustainable. The US Government (as well as most of the governments of western Europe) is not operating in a fiscally sustainable fashion. The problem is simple: we are spending too much, and there is no overall process in place to limit the spending to match reasonable tax receipts.

The solution to sustainability is staring us in the face. We need what Ronald Reagan asked for 30 years ago – a balanced budget amendment. There will be pain in adapting to a new world order in which we (only) spend 2 trillion dollars a year as opposed to 3. But we will live. And after that, we will prosper like never before.

8. Healthcare, Simplified

SO FAR, WE HAVE OUTLINED THE *BROAD STROKES* OF HOW TO THINK OF AN IDEAL 21RST GOVERNMENT. The process should be brought online, with electronic accounts, electronic voting and online records; taxes should be dramatically simplified; a balanced budget amendment should be passed and simple procedures and straightforward accounting should be put in place to actually start balancing it.

We have also reviewed a century of economic thought and economic history; we've made the case that in general free markets work substantially better than central planning, and that we need a leaner, more efficient, *less complex* government. But we haven't gone into specific areas of government activity or spend.

We will now address the single largest growing, most complex, and most broken area of all – healthcare. Its not only an enormous part of our government spend, it's an enormous part of our entire economy. As a percentage of GDP, healthcare costs have has risen steadily from 4.6% in 1960 (when I was born) to 9% in 1980 to 17% in 2012. And two thirds of this massive (and growing) burden on the economy is now being funded by federal, state and local governments.

In real terms, the economy has grown 4 times since 1960; 2 times on a per capita basis. On that same per-capita basis, healthcare spending is now 6 times, again, *after* adjusting for inflation. This is not a question of the government "doing something about healthcare" – it's a question of the government "something *else*". We can simply not afford the system as it stands.

For all this spending, our system barely works: 60% of all bankruptcies are medical-related, and 70% of those involve patients *with* insurance. Emergency room lines are longer than ever, hospitals have fewer beds per patient visit, and doctors no longer make house calls.

And people are not getting any healthier – on the contrary, obesity rates and diabetes have both doubled during that period. Abuse of anti-depressants, and painkillers are rampant, particularly among teenagers and younger children. Of all aspects of government, this could be the biggest failure.

Three key groups control the process: the insurance companies, the hospitals, and state claims processes – which are themselves primarily funded from federal dollars. Medical equipment vendors, big Pharma and the FDA approval process also play significant roles. It's a very a complicated web of interests, but there are some clear simplifications that can be made.

Our recommendations are as follows:

- Make this a federal problem, not a state one. The idea of raising money at the national level and then dispersing it to various states for claims re-imbursement makes no sense.

- Provide close to free, basic, national, guaranteed healthcare coverage for every single American. There should be a small deductible for every single doctor visit, procedure, or medical prescription -- but there should be a baseline healthcare option that is simple, and nationwide.

- For the near-free baseline, severely limit the amount of completely covered medical procedures. In many instances, for example, MRI's are not *necessary*, they are simply *desirable*. Patients should be able to elect to upgrade to an MRI, a revolutionary new cancer drug, or a proton ray treatment, but they should pay for the upgrade.

- Make it easier for customers to shop for medical care alternatives, both for baseline health services and for optional upgrades. Eliminate state and federal regula-tions on new, innovative healthcare companies com-peting against the bloated hospital system.

- Require that hospitals and insurance companies share patient data with the patients. Right now, only 25% of all hospitals use digital records – and most of the ones that are keep the information siloed in doctors hands. This data needs to be transportable and accessible by patients.

- Incentivize health and wellness. Insurance companies discriminate against obese people and smokers. The government should as well. It is unacceptable that the fit amongst us pay for the bad habits of the rest. We can even go further and fund not only health *care* but wellness, fitness, nutrition and physical training. It is cheaper to keep people healthy than to treat chronic disease.

- Encourage efficiency and specialization amongst healthcare providers. We need the "Starbucks" of MRI's, the Henry Ford of bypass operations, The $99 "Jiffy Lube" 30 minute doctor checkups. For this, we need less red tape and regulations, and an openness to new ideas.

Healthcare is a National Issue

At the time the United States was founded, in 1776, the concept of providing healthcare benefits (or any other paid benefits) from national coffers to private citizens would never have been considered seriously. Moreover, there was a clear distinction between federal expenditures (having an army, maintaining a justice system etc..) and state ones (education, roads, mail etc..).

Two hundred years later, basic healthcare is generally perceived as a type of birthright worldwide. Part of this is due to a general rise in living standards; in a world where we have an abundance of food, billionaires, advanced medical technology and atomic energy it seems *unfair* that people should suffer or die simply for financial reasons. And, most people would also agree that some form of basic healthcare support is *in their own best interests*. No matter who you are, there is always a possibility that you yourself will need that support somewhere down the road.

For historical reasons, the way this has been addressed up until now has been to levy taxes to pay for these healthcare benefits at the federal level, but then makes grants to individual states in the form of Medicare and over a hundred other programs.

As the Cato Institute points out, this is highly inefficient:

> "Federal aid is an inefficient way to fund state and local activities. It encourages overspending by the states, comes with complex federal regulations that stifle innovation, and generates bureaucracies at all levels of government. Americans would have more frugal, transparent, and responsible government if aid programs were eliminated. There are no advantages of funding state and local activities with federal dollars, but there are many disadvantages to the economy and to sound governance."

Making healthcare a national issue does not mean that we need a system such as France's or the UK's where everything is covered, your choices of providers is low, and the overall cost to the economy is (like ours) enormous. It only means that we should centralize the claims process, substituting one national system for fifty state ones.

The Legacy of State Laws

Like all overly complex systems, our current state-based healthcare system has significant disadvantages over a simpler, centralized one.

To begin with, different state laws mean that you have to sign up for a different insurance company every time you move states. Blue Cross of California does not translate into Blue Cross of Oregon – they are distinct, separate companies, with different requirements.

Because an insurance plan from one state can't compete with an insurance company in the state next door, consumers have fewer options, and their insurance prices are significantly higher than they should be. And there are less possibilities for real economies of scale nationwide. Imagine if Wal-Mart or Whole Foods were prohibited from operating in multiple states and you get an idea of the problems innovative healthcare companies face.

These issues are compounded by the advent of the Internet. While you can't (yet) get a diagnosis entirely online, many aspects of the healthcare process have moved to the cloud -- including the fast growing area of medical imaging. As Jonathan Bush notes with amazement[24]

> "in cloud based diagnostic centers today each image must only be entrusted to experts licensed in the state where the patient lives"

No doubt, the insurance companies and hospitals will lobby to prevent any loosening up of these archaic state laws. The last thing they want is a national simplification and re-think of the entire process.

The Size of The Problem

Health Care now represents about a sixth of our overall economy, and is rising as a share every year.

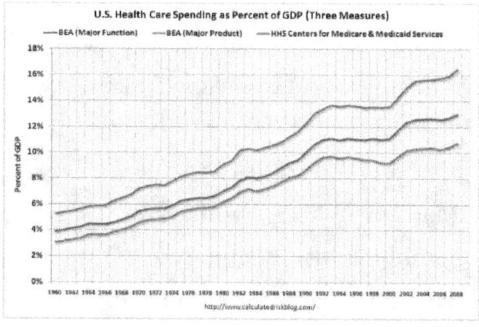

Figure 8 Growth of US Heath Care as a Percentage of GDP

In 1966, the topline metric was 6% of GDP. Today we are 2.5x that – at 16%. If this trend continues (and it could), fifty years from now half of the entire economy will be spent on healthcare.

The United States spends significantly more, per capita, than any other country, as the table below illustrates:

OECD (2011)[1]

Rank	Country	Total health expenditure per capita PPP US$	Total health expenditure % of GDP
1	United States	8,508	17.7
2	Norway	5,669	9.3
3	Switzerland	5,643	11.0
4	Netherlands	5,099	11.9
5	Austria	4,546	10.8
6	Canada	4,522	11.2
7	Germany	4,495	11.3
8	Denmark	4,448	10.9
9	Luxembourg	4,246	6.6
10	France	4,118	11.6
11	Belgium	4,061	10.5
12	Sweden	3,925	9.5
13	Australia	3,800 (2010)	8.9 (2010)

Figure 9 Healthcare as a Percentage of GDP. OECD Countries.

This data will surprise some people. The fact that we spend twice as much on per capita as Sweden, and almost twice as much as France – two countries with very high consumer satisfaction ratings in the healthcare department – proves that we are doing something wrong.

Zero Incentives to Cut Costs

The main problem of the current US Healthcare system is that nowhere is there any incentive to cut cost. An example described by Jonathan Bush illustrates this perfectly; consider the modern wonder of the proton ray gun – a tool that uses a rarely found particle in nature, a proton (the opposite of an electron) to make extremely complex surgical incisions. Because of the complexity and high-tech nature of the proton gun, a single treatment costs as much as $32,000 – and as an ideal method of colonoscopy. On the other hand, an older treatment called IMRT provides in almost all cases near identical results at a fraction of the cost. Both procedures are 100% covered by insurance plans – and by Medicare. Guess which one ends up getting selected in a head-head competition.

Because the current system does not incentivize patients for selecting better value treatments (as opposed to just better treatments) there is no notion of "shopping." And because there is no shopping, there is little incentive for any new entrepreneurial company to try to provide better solutions for todays problems at a better cost.

In his key book "The Innovator's Dilemma", Harvard MBS Professor Clay Christianson identified that type of entrepreneurial activity as being the key ingredient for technological progress. In case after case, innovation in semi-conductors, software, disk drives, memory, computers and other fields started with creating a worse product, but at massively cheaper prices. That feature-poorer product does not appeal to the top third of the market, but is "good enough" for the bottom two thirds and finds early adoption. Eventually features and functionality get added so that the technology becomes the new standard; and the process starts all over.

Without the ability of consumers to benefit by choosing *inferior*, but *cheaper* medical solutions this model for innovation cannot take place. Instead, we have a different more IBM Mainframe / Oracle model that is typified by large, closed enterprise medical software systems such as "Epic[25]" that costs tens of millions of dollars, and requires thousands of highly paid consultants to set up. In the 1960's "nobody got fired for buying IBM"; fifty years later the same is true with Epic in the medical records business.

Cover The Basics and Encourage Shopping

How do you incentivize and reward consumers for saving money on healthcare? One way would be to actually pay them back a percentage of the money they save the system. Need a colonoscopy? It's covered, and you have the choice of the Proton Gun, or the IMRT. But if you choose the IMRT, you also get $5,000 in cash. Even with the cash payment, this solution would save the government (and the economy) a boatload. But obviously paying people cash payments for choosing lower quality services every time they fall sick somehow seems wrong, and could be itself subject to abuse.

A better solution is simply to cover the basics – and allow the patient to upgrade at his or her own expense to a more "Rolls Royce" treatment.

When people are spending their own money, as opposed to someone else's they make better shopping decisions (see the Friedman Matrix in Chapter 4). The government should cover basic healthcare needs, providing a bare-bones level of support that is sufficient for people with no financial resources. But people with greater financial resources should be able to use that same support, plus their own funds and upgrade to the level of healthcare service that makes sense *for them.*

By encouraging consumers to make better medical services (and product) buying decisions, you are also encouraging entrepreneurs and companies to come in and provide those services and products. Take for example the case of MRI imaging. Today, as noted by Jonathan Bush, prices for an MRI scan range from $3,000 to $6,000. There is no incentive for hospitals to provide them at any lower price, as the cost is 100% covered by insurance. If it was only partially covered, however, there would be a strong incentive for MRI imaging centers to be created all over the country. MRI machines can be rented for as little as $8,000 a month per machine. Bush estimates that the wholesale cost of an MRI scan could be brought down to $28 – allowing a good profit margin to be realized even at a price point as low as $99 per scan – a 30x savings!

Vouchers and Consumer Choice

The actual implementation of incentives is tricky. Republicans rightly cringe at the thought of having their healthcare options taken away from them. Who in the middle class wants to be told that they must use the communal facilities, or pay 100% of it themselves? It's a bad deal for everybody who can afford more than the minimum level of service, and it creates two separate classes of patients – those on the take, and those who pay twice; once for themselves and once for the others.

A better solution is to give people vouchers that they can use for basic treatment, or use as partial payment for more elaborate treatment. This allows people to pick their own healthcare providers, and select exactly where on the spectrum of treatments they want to be (for any specific occasion or disease).

The Buffet Model

Lee Kwan Yu, the founder of modern day Singapore, has been a long time critic of western "all-you-can-eat" healthcare models. He compares it to a mediocre hotel buffet, and notes the incentive to over-indulge.

> "Much happens with all you can eat health care. People have severely limited choices and the service is mediocre, but they consume a lot of health care."

If you never see a bill, you don't care what it costs. That applies to doctors as well as patients. And as a provider, you don't particularly care about quality; people will show up at your buffet whether the food is good or not. No need to build a great product or company, no need to innovate, no need to provide anything but basic service.

Compare this to Fast Med Urgent Care, a "Starbucks for Urgent Care" started in North Carolina. With fast service, clear pricing at $59, $79 and $99, Fast Med is the type of company the government should encourage by incentivizing choice and competition. In 2013 Fast med was the fastest growing privately owned company in North Carolina.

The Role of Private Insurance

A national health policy, and direct reimbursement of medical claims at the federal level does not preclude in any way the participation of private insurance. But it should not be necessary. Like France, the UK or Sweden, a person should be able to never *have to* deal with a private healthcare insurance company in their life. Companies should not be forced to offer health insurance to their employees – the government should do that.

Instead, insurance companies should be allowed to operate and compete nationwide, offering supplemental insurance of various kinds to individuals, companies and families who wish to go beyond the basic US government package. Increased competition will break what is now a very profitable (for the insurance companies) oligopoly. With the government insurance as a backstop, these companies will have less of an opportunity to gouge patients. Even foreign insurance companies should be allowed to compete; less barriers and more entrants is the simple key to lower prices and better service.

Transportable Data

Amazingly, only a quarter of all hospitals have digital records of their patients. We all know the sinking feeling of finding a new doctor or hospital, and filling out 6 pages of patient data that clearly should exist in the cloud, and be transferable, at the patients option to a chosen service provider.

Similarly, patients don't have access to their own medical files. If a doctor writes something in your file, not only can no other doctor typically see it, you can't either.

This is a basic data entry problem, a standards problem, and a legal problem. The federal government should set open, uniform standards for how this data should be stored, how to request it, and how to deal with breaches in security, which of course also occur with physical files. The legal risks of "transmitting vital and confidential information over the Internet" are a smokescreen; the reality is very few players are incented to move to digital, and many have a direct interest in maintaining the status quo.

There should be a patient bill of rights that makes medical records freely transportable. Large medical systems companies such as Epic (the IBM of Medical Systems) should be required to provide this data via secure API's to other service providers, technology companies and ultimately individual patients.

In the future, wearable and implantable devices will continuously record our vital stats, including weight, body fat, pulse, blood pressure, physical activity levels, sleep, blood sugar levels, and abnormal organ activity. Fed into a network of medical analysis systems, and compared against past history, this data will alert service providers to problems even before they occur. Keeping this data "provider neutral" will become an issue in the 21rst century.

Our Nutrition Problem

A discussion of healthcare cannot be complete without a discussion of one of the root causes of many of our diseases: obesity. As the following graphs show, we as a nation (and as a planet) are becoming increasingly overweight.

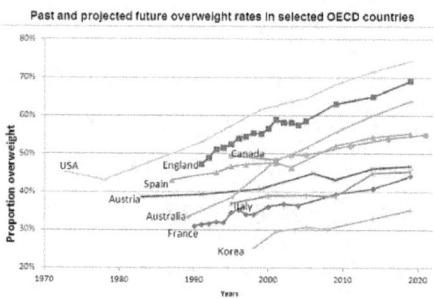

Figure 10 Growth of Obesity in OECD Countries

Obesity rates have doubled in every single major industrial-ized nation since 1980. Furthermore, in a study by the Center for Disease Control[26], we are gaining on average half a pound per year, every year, on average. The study concludes that

- The average weight for men rose "dramatically", from 166.3 pounds in 1960 to 191 pounds in 2002. Women went from 140.2 pounds in 1960 to 164.3 pounds in 2002.

- Weight increases were greater among older men. Those between 40 and 49 were nearly 27 pounds heavier on average at the end of the study period. Men 50 to 59 got 28 pounds heavier, and 60 to 74 were almost 33 pounds heavier on average in 2002 compared with 1960

Every single state is affected – with the "Red States" being the worse hit. Obesity rates in the south and Midwest are now close to 30%.

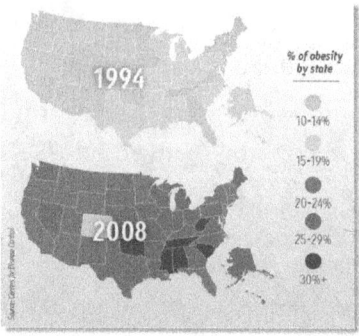

Figure 11 Obesity By State. The Red States are the most obese.

One of the immediate causes is Diabetes, which is now reaching epidemic proportions:

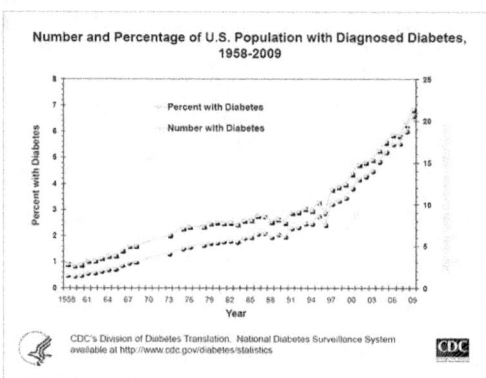

Figure 12 Growth of Diabetes since 1958.

Diabetes rates have tripled since the 1970's! 6% of the American Population now has Diabetes.

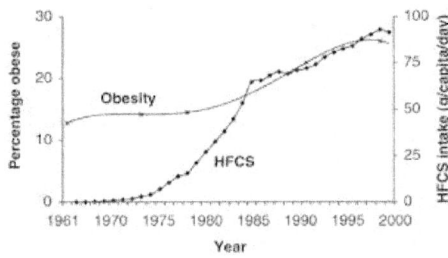

Figure 13 Correlation between HFCS and Obesity

One of the major culprits is High Fructose Corn Syrups (HFCS) – the main sweetener found in soft drinks, and a primary ingredient in packaged and fast food. Correlation does not equal causality, but the data does point to HFCS as one of the main drivers of our weight epidemic. We will get into this later, but for now, lets just summarize as follows:

> The US (as rest of the world as well) is becoming severely unhealthy. The cost of treating this is now one of the largest components of the government budget.

The solution to this problem is not more government spending on medical benefits or prescription drugs. It is, simply put, to encourage people to become more healthy. A combination of incentives and a simplification of the coverage system can do this.

Incentivizing Wellness

Many of American's medical problems can be directly diagnosed to lifestyle factors, nutrition being front and center. If the nation as a whole had not (partially) taken on the cost of overall healthcare, it could be argued that this is the government meddling with private citizen's affairs. But when you smoke, become obese, or completely ignore your own fitness, *and* claim medical benefits, you are abusing the system.

A number of different solutions to this have been proposed in the past, including a highly controversial "Fat Tax."[27] I would like to instead propose a more positive "badge system" with cash rewards, inspired by the achievement badges of apps such as FitBit[28] and Nike FuelBand[29].

Just like non-smokers and non-obese people get discounts with certain HMOs (including Kaiser Permanente) and insurance companies, the government could offer small cash rewards (potentially on the order of $1,000 per person per year) for achieving standardized age-defined levels of fitness. Over and above the cash incentive, these badges could enter our collective culture as a "good thing to have", in much the same way that a college degree is a mark of achievement.

Another cost-effective measure would be to cover wellness costs as well as disease treatment costs. Basic physical training and gyms could be 100% covered by the state once accredited. Individuals could opt to smoothly upgrade to better, more individualized plans at their own costs, but they would benefit from partial reimbursement.

Adding a comprehensive wellness program to our healthcare efforts simply makes sense. We need to look after our citizens in the same way a company looks after its employees.

Healthy, active citizens will make America stronger. And studies have shown that physical health promotes mental health and better thinking. In the new global information economy we need as sharp and healthy a labor force as we can get.

Finally, as mentioned above fast food, high fructose corn syrup, soft drinks, cigarettes and cigars are all the enemy. Like New York City's mayor Bloomberg, the federal government should consider further excise taxes, calorie warnings, and other labeling requirement to discourage their use. Obviously, this would be fought tooth and nail by companies with a vested interest in keeping us unhealthy. Olson's law again applies. But if it can work for NY City, it can work for the country. We just need strong leadership and a general recognition that change is necessary.

Specialization

One of the most promising developments in healthcare is the possibility of dramatically reducing costs by specializing treatment. A leading country here, surprisingly, is India. Another is Sweden.

Consider Dr. Devi Shetty's Heart Bypass Clinic[30]. With over 1,000 beds this clinic is significantly larger than most American general purpose hospitals (160 beds), but only does one thing: heart bypass operations. By performing these operations in an assembly line fashion, with surgeons working continuously as opposed to in spurts, Shetty has reduced the cost of a bypass from the US Rate of $100,000 to just $2,000.

In Sweden, a private equity firm, Capio[31] has taken over a 300 bed hospital and is applying similar modern, factory automation principles. This "lean healthcare" model has dramatically reduced waiting times, and unnecessary examinations. The hospital "scorecard" is published on the Capio intranet on a daily basis; management by objectives has resulted in an overall "98% quality score."

Similar facilities could exist in the US, especially if we get rid of obsolete state requirements, and state insurance plans. A center in Kansas, for example, would be an easy three hour plane ride from anywhere in the country; a cost effective facility could actually buy jets and fly people in for treatment and still save money.

Medical image processing could be done in low cost, single purpose facilities miles away from the actual patient. They could even be done overseas, in cost effective countries such as the Philippines. The single goal should be to cut costs and deliver a superior product to the end user. Apple makes its computers and phones in China; we should be fine if a qualified worker in a foreign country processes an x-ray, or enhances an MRI image.

End of Life Treatment

One of the most politicized and difficult areas of healthcare policy is coverage during the last few months of a person's life. It is a fact of the current system that 50% of the average person's healthcare costs occur in his or her last 90 days.

It is a difficult subject, because it requires us to deal, squarely with the very simple fact that we all die. Deciding not to perform an operation that could keep someone alive versus dying on the spot seems philosophically untenable, but in point of fact, it happens every day – we just choose to ignore it.

Offering a simple, humane, but cost effective end-of-life treatment to everybody should be the goal. If certain rich individuals or individuals with generous families want to extend their lives beyond the "basic program", they should do it at their own cost. Already, today rich patients like Steve Jobs can get life saving organ transplants and specialized treatment which are not available to the general public. This is not a case of wanting to resurrect the "death squads" that plagued the Obama presidential campaign.[32]

Healthcare Simplified -- Summary.

You cannot simplify government without simplifying healthcare. Despite the scope of the problem, it is fixable with only short term pain; if we take the medicine the medium and long term prospects actually look good.

First and foremost we need to tackle this problem on a national level, and cover a basic minimum directly, without dealing with the individual states or individual insurance companies. Like welfare and education, the solution is to provide the bare minimum, but include a clear upgrade path that incentivizes shopping and choice.

9. A Simpler Safety Net

WE HAVE COVERED THE HISTORICAL GROWTH OF THE WELFARE STATE IN CHAPTER 5, and the size and scope of the healthcare sub-system in Chapter 8. We now turn to one of the most polarizing topics around: assistance to the poor, unfortunate, disabled and elderly.

Everybody has an opinion on this subject, and these opinions are often of the knee-jerk variety. Your rich republican uncle has probably told you that "the bums should get a job", while your best friend's wife is outraged that poverty even exists in the 21rst century. Can we say anything at all on this subject without crossing political demarcation lines?

We think so. In this chapter we will argue that the entire system of providing resources to those in need can be dramatically simplified. We don't need 100 separate programs for the unemployed, the retired, the disabled, and those people with chronic conditions. We don't need social security, with its own arcane (and bankrupt) accounting system. We just need a clear and efficient way to provide cash to those in need and incentivize them to participate in the labor force in either a part time or full time capacity.

A simplification of the entire process means less programs to administer, less government staff needed to administer them, and less loopholes for people who really don't need government aid. It also means that the welfare state, as we know it, can actually shrink. This is not a case of the rich getting more and the poor getting less; it's a case of re-organizing the store so that everybody finds what they want more easily, and that we are all excited and incented to contribute.

The Current Scope of the Welfare State

There is a simple reason that the we need reform: the welfare state has become enormous beyond belief. As the Heritage Foundation[33] (a conservative think tank) points out:

> "According to the nonpartisan Congressional Research Service (CRS) shows the staggering reality of the growing welfare state — and reveals welfare spending is approaching the $1 trillion mark.

> Roughly 100 million people—one-third of the U.S. population—receive aid from at least one means-tested welfare program each month. Average benefits come to around $9,000 per recipient. If converted to cash, means-tested welfare spending is more than five times the amount needed to eliminate all poverty in the United States."

As much as we might like to, we simply don't have the money to continue funding this kind of spending. To make matters worse, the numbers are headed up, not down.

As the following chart shows, total federal and state spending on Welfare has increased from 50 Billion to 1 Trillion, or 20x in the last 50 years. The amazing thing about this chart (and I had to go back and verify it) *is that the numbers are indeed inflation adjusted.*

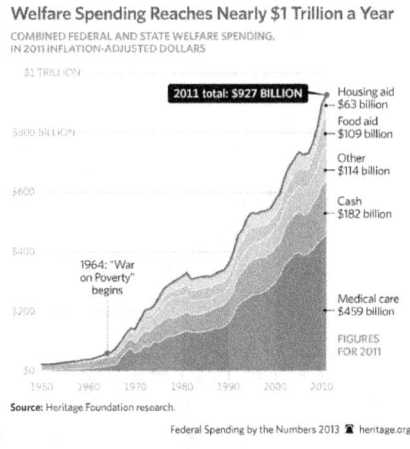

Welfare Spending Reaches Nearly $1 Trillion a Year

COMBINED FEDERAL AND STATE WELFARE SPENDING,
IN 2011 INFLATION-ADJUSTED DOLLARS

2011 total: $927 BILLION

Housing aid
$63 billion

Food aid
$109 billion

Other
$114 billion

Cash
$182 billion

1964: "War
on Poverty"
begins

Medical care
$459 billion

FIGURES
FOR 2011

Source: Heritage Foundation research.

Federal Spending by the Numbers 2013 ☎ heritage.org

Figure 14 Growth of The Welfare state.

It seems absolutely mind-boggling that real welfare payments could have increased 20 times since I was born, but that in fact, is the case. Again, quoting the Heritage Foundation,

> "In 1965 when Lyndon Johnson launched the War on poverty, aggregate welfare spending was only $8.9 billion. (This would amount to around $42 billion if adjusted for inflation into today's dollars.)"

In nominal terms, welfare spending has increased 100x

The Problems with Our Current System

There are two fundamental problems with our current welfare system:

- It is not adequately restricted to people in need.
- There are not good incentives for people to get off the system.

The first point is a direct consequence of the systems complexity. With multiple programs, many savvy individuals have found ways to receive overlapping benefits, or benefits they don't deserve.

Disability Fraud

In 2013 60 Minutes ran a segment[34] on the abuse of disability payments that is well worth watching.

The Federal Disability Insurance Program[35] is part of the Social Security program and was set up in the 1950s to help people who were unable to work because of illness or injury. It was originally thought of as a small program – the statutes read that if you are only eligible if you cannot work at all – but today 12 million people are on it, and it costs 135 billion dollars, almost a full percentage of our GDP.

A random survey of disability files by ranking republican Tom Colburn from Oklahoma showed 25% clearly should not have been approved, and another 25% were highly questionable. That level of fraud is simply outrageous. And it is being perpetuated by professional law firms such as Binder and Binder[36] who represent claimants on a success fee basis. The system is being gamed.

Gaming aside, the current disability system does little to get people back to work. By definition, in order to collect disability, you need to be *off work*, and there is no incentive to re-train or add incremental jobs. A better system would be Denmark's where disability grants are only given if your work is permanently impaired and if you cannot even accept flexible work options.

Welfare that Exceeds Entry Level Jobs

As the Cato institute points the blame squarely on welfare programs that exceed, in terms of after tax benefits, the kind of entry-level jobs that welfare recipients are likely to qualify for.

> "One of the single best ways to climb out of poverty is taking a job, but as long as welfare provides a better standard of living than an entry-level job, recipients will continue to choose it over work," said Michael Tanner, senior policy analyst

and   co-author   of   the   study.

Welfare recipients in Hawaii get the most benefits, according to Tanner, at $29.13 per hour — or $60,590 pre-tax income annually. However, the state's minimum wage is only $7.25 per hour, according to the Labor Department. Hawaiians on welfare also earn 167 percent of the median salary in the state, which is only $36,275."

A Single Program

Taking Healthcare benefits out of the 1 Trillion dollars a year of spend of "means tested welfare programs" still leaves close to 400 billion dollars a year of benefits distributed across literally hundreds of programs. With social security, which in theory is meant to provide retirement benefits for lower income workers, the number is closer to 1.5 Trillion.

The great simplification is to group all these recipients in a common category, and reduce all these programs to one. Rather than have a separate program for the disabled, another one for unemployed families, another one for retired workers, food stamp programs, housing assistance programs and programs for veterans, we can have a simple monthly cash payment that is solely dependent on income levels – and payable at the federal, not the state level.

That payment should be incrementally additive to any other sources of income the person receives. For example, take an unemployed 20 year old college student with no children. Regardless of the state that this person lives in, he or she would be entitled to a base (taxable) payment of $1,000 a month. After tax, the person would take home $800 a month.

Now assume the same person was able to make an additional $1,000 a month working part time (for example, tutoring). According to a simple formula, the stipend would decrease smoothly down to $800. The student would now be earning $1,800 a month, or $1,400 a month after the 20% flat tax. The more the college student works, the higher his or her after tax income. There is a clear incentive to not live entirely off welfare.

The same logic applies whether we are talking about an individual, a family, a disabled person, a veteran or a retiree. The amount of the stipend would be different if the person has a number of dependents (the poverty line depends on the family size), but it would not be sufficient to encourage people to have children for the mere sake of getting welfare payments.

It would also be the same across all states – encouraging people to move to states with a lower cost of living. It is true that $1,000 a month does not go far in New York City, but it is a livable salary in Kansas.

Social Security

The original point of social security was need to provide *some* retirement assistance to low income elderly workers. The program is however, technically bankrupt. There is no way that the funds collected by social security withholdings will be sufficient to cover the obligations as set forth in the original plan. Rather than try to fix it, we should recognize that it simply doesn't work and terminate it – dealing with the problem of poor retirees in the same blanket way described above.

Of course, many beneficiaries of Social Security (and other welfare benefits) are not actually people in need. Warren Buffet and Bill Gates both are entitled to social security, as an extreme example. Given that we clearly can't afford the program, replacing it with a simple welfare payment that only applies to low income earners makes more sense.

This was the point of Social Security. We can call it something else, fund it differently, but we need to take care of our retirees – to the extent that private system does not. Similarly, if you are out of work and cannot find work, the state should provide a minimum amount of support. We can (and will) debate how much, and in what form – but the general concept is indisputable. Finally, if you experience a catastrophic illness, and do not have the means to pay, it seems only reasonable that the state should cover it. People dying in the street is not an option.

Other than defense, this idea of a "safety net" is one of key functions of modern government. Unfortunately, it is one of the most poorly executed and abused. Some quick facts illustrate the problem clearly:

- Social Security as a program is technically bankrupt, but meanwhile is being used to make the deficit look better than it actually is.

- Welfare and medical entitlements have grown 20x in real (inflation adjusted dollars) since the 1960s. Half the country does not pay taxes, a third of the country actually *lives off of welfare.*

- As a country, we spend significantly more per capita on medical care than even countries such as France or Denmark – with universally recognized horrific results

What we need to solve this issue is reduced welfare benefits and clear incentives to both supplement, and eventually replace welfare with work

Immigration And Welfare

A commonly held belief, especially amongst republicans, but also among very sizable numbers of democrats, is that many of our budget problems are due to the cost of supporting illegal aliens on welfare. The argument plays well to xenophobic and racist pre-conceptions, but is not grounded in reality (at least for the US). As the libertarian Cato Institute points out[37]:

> "In a new paper, we show that, historically, immigrants and their descendants have not increased the

size of individual welfare benefits or welfare budgets and are unlikely to do so going forward. The amount of welfare benefits is unaffected by the foreign origin or diversity of the population.

Since 1970, no pattern can be seen between the size of benefits a family of three gets under welfare programs like *Temporary Aid for Needy Families* (TANF) and the level of immigration or ethnic and racial diversity."

Every single high tech company I am aware of is in favor of relaxed immigration policies. Reforming welfare does not mean closing our borders; both Texas and Florida have shown that welfare growth can be contained even with high degrees of immigration.

A Simpler Safety Net -- Summary

A good government takes care of its people. But it does not do so at the expense of its general sustainability, or by severely limiting its overall growth rate. We can provide a simpler safety net without creating a nation dependent on welfare, and dis-incentivized to get back to work. The key in all cases is to provide a minimum support level dependent only on income. As people take extra side jobs, and eventually full time jobs, their take home pay should always go in one direction: up.

With the right safety net in place the US can once again become a welcoming nation for foreign talent.

10. A Reasonable Defense

THE COUNTRY NEEDS A STRONG DEFENSE, BUT NOT A DEFENSE AT ALL COSTS. So how big is our current defense – and can we cut back?

The table below shows the 2012 data on Military Expenditure as a % of GDP for the top world powers:

United States:	640 Billion	3.8%
China:	188 Billion	2.0%
Russia:	87 Billion	4.1%
Saudi Arabia:	67 Billion	2.2%
France:	61 Billion	2.1%

It's clear that the US is spending far more than any other country at the present time. This is certainly not a new trend. Historically, defense as a % of GDP is between 4% and 6% and, since 1989, in the even narrower 4%-5% range.

Let's point out however, the US is not at war. Even we spent *half* of the amount we are currently spending, we would still outspend Russia and China combined.

The fact that US Defense Spending has been so big for so long does not prove in any way that it is at the optimal level.

Clearly (thank goodness) we are no longer in an arms race with Russia. Relative to the next superpower – China – we have 20 times as many nuclear weapons as the table below shows:

Russia: 8,500 Nukes

USA: 7,700 Nukes

France: 300 Nukes

China: 250 Nukes

Looking at a different metric, the number of Aircraft Carriers, we see a similar pattern

USA: 10 Aircraft Carriers

China: 1 Aircraft Carrier

Russia: 1 Aircraft Carrier

Regarding Nuclear Subs, the same pattern holds:

USA: 71 Nuclear Subs

Russia: 33 Nuclear Subs

China: 10 Nuclear Subs

It is easy to say that "there is no price for security" – but the reality is that our biggest weakness today is economic security – not military security. Even if we *doubled* the size of our military budget it would not do much to stop an isolated terrorist from creating a mass attack of violence; on the other hand, the entire system came close to a financial meltdown just 5 years ago because of an out-of-control banking system.

The fact is that spending growth is unsustainable, and most reasonable people agree that the military budget must be reined in. In May 2012 the Henry L. Stimson Center, a non-partisan Washington, D.C., think tank, released the results of a survey which showed the majority of democrat, republican and independent voters want to cut military spending more severely than either party has proposed.

Former presidential candidate Ron Paul brought up the issue during a debate in Tampa, Fla., in September 2011. "We're under great threat, because we occupy so many countries," he said at the time. "We're in 130 countries. We have 900 bases around the world. We're going broke."

Nukes and The Department of Energy

Amazingly, the nation's nuclear arsenal is not even under the control of the military, but under the Department of Energy. The entire nuclear weapons program, including the nuclear reactor production for the US Navy and the disposal of radioactive waste falls within that $28 Billion budget (in fact, represents the majority of that budget). This is just another example of misleading high level government accounting.

Defense versus Foreign Intervention

One of the main problems with the word "Defense" is that it masks activities that in fact don't relate to the *protection* of our country, but rather seek to further economic or other agendas. This makes it very difficult to talk about a "Defense Budget". As the Cato Institute points out:

> "In a literal sense, the United States does not have a defense budget. The adjective is wrong. Our military spending is for many purposes: other nations' defense, the purported extension of freedom, the maintenance of hegemony, and the ability to threaten any other nation with conquest. But the relationship between these objectives and the end they purport to serve, the protection of Americans and their welfare, is unclear. In fact, defining the requirements of our defense so broadly is probably counterproductive. Our global military posture and activism drag us into others' conflicts, provoke animosity, cause states to balance our power, and waste resources. We need a defense budget worthy of the name."

George Bush's 6 Trillion Invasion of Iraq[38] clearly, in hindsight, can hardly be considered "Defense". Nor can these expenses be justified by a new "war on terrorism." That kind of "war" by definition will involve more intelligence gather-

ing, and small surgical strikes as opposed to large convention-
al troop operations.

Relax, We are Safe

The political way Washington deals with budget crises is to
set hard caps on spending by agency, without specifying
where the cuts are coming from, and then decry any actual
measures to reduce spending. With defense, this kind of dou-
ble-talk is coming from both the right and the left. Obama's
proposed 2015 military budget is a case in point; the same
people who approved the high-level figures are lamenting that
the cuts are going to "slash" our military and hurt our security. None of this is true.

With over 450,000 active troops, plus a growing Special Ops
Force estimated to hit 70,000 the army cannot be reasonably
accused of being "gutted." Furthermore, as the Benjamin
Friedman of the Cato Institute notes[39],

> No U.S. enemy has the capability to take advantage
> of the proposed reductions. Russia's foray in Cri-
> mea had nothing to do with the U.S. Army's size.
> The capability to bomb Iran, Syria or North Korea
> remains, even simultaneously. A few less ships
> barely affect the massive superiority our Navy
> would enjoy against China in the East Pacific.

One actual benefit of a simpler, smaller army is that it makes another invasion like Iraq less likely. Huge standing armies can tempt a president into foreign intervention; the people are in place anyways, so why not use them?

Exposing The Hidden Costs of War

When George W. Bush lobbied congress on his decision to invade Iraq, he downplayed some estimates that the war would cost upwards of $200 Billion, insisting that $50 Billion was all that he would need. In the end, the war ended up costing an estimated $6 Trillion dollars – with Joseph E. Stieglitz estimating *veterans benefits alone* at $1 Trillion.

These kind of "mistakes" are hard to comprehend. Part of it seems due to the fact many costs are not accrued in advance[40], and are only recognized when they actually occur. In the case of long term disability, the bulk of these costs can happen decades after the actual war.

Furthermore as mentioned in the previous section, there is an accounting fallacy that the forces needed to fight the war are "all paid for." In point of fact, there is a clear opportunity cost to actually reducing the size of the military.

A long term target of 2% of GDP

Milton Friedman once remarked[41] that he had never met a government official that said that the problem was *too much* government spending. We are sure that this is true of Pentagon officials as well. But the simple fact of the matter is that China, France, and Britain are all currently just 2% of their GDP on Defense while we are spending double that.

The United States benefits from having two friendly neighbors, with two massive oceans on either side of us. The cold war and the arms race with Russia is over, our position in the world is converging to equality with China on one hand and Europe on the other. There is simply no good reason to maintain the kind of arsenal we have today at the cost of economic ruin.

From a pure accounting point of view the government should consolidate veteran's affairs, defense, homeland security and national intelligence under a single line item, and report that item clearly and transparently to taxpayers. Over a 4 year period, we should bring this budget inline with the 2% number. If that means less foreign intervention, less nuclear weapons, and less veterans with disabilities, that is a good thing.

A Reasonable Defense – Summary.

We are not experts on military armament costs, nor on the geopolitical military realities that confront the oval office. But it is clear that the United States military is spending far more than it needs to currently, and has been doing so for a very long time. One of things that brings down empires is overreach. It is high time we checked our international ambitions and concentrated first and foremost on solving our domestic economic problems.

11. Education, Revisited.

ONE OF THE LARGEST EXPENSES OF ALL MOD-
ERN SOCIETIES IS EDUCATION. In the case of the
United States, about 5.4% of our GDP is spent on public
schools. That number is roughly correct; it is not the case that
we are investing far too much, or too little on the next generation. But the allocation and organization of that spend could
be simplified and improved.

This chapter will make the case that the concept of charter
schools should be expanded and broadened to become the
default for all K-12 education. Certainly, charter schools are a
competitive threat for the obsolete public school system, and
for existing teachers unions. But giving parents more choice
in where to educate their children is the long term key concept to improving learning in the 21rst century – not centrally
planned curriculums and one-size-fits all high school programs.

We shouldn't be debating, like Lynne Cheney did in 1994[42]
the relative importance of Paul Revere and the Ku Klux Klan
in US History. It is perfectly fine that some schools focus on
our revolutionary heroes while others teach our children
about the darker side of our past. Not everybody needs to
vanilla ice cream; some of us prefer chocolate or pistachio. I

am not a Mormon, but I have no problem allocating government money to support Mormon public education in Salt Lake City – as long as quantitative testing proves that the education is worthwhile.

As a country, however, there are certain skills that we clearly need more of, and these should be incentivized, over, for example Mormon Bible study achievement, or even US History. Math, Science, Information Technology and Medicine are a few of the obvious growth areas of the future. We should incentivize, recognize and award achievement in these areas. This could and should be done at the Federal Level.

Finally, we will take a serious and long look at online education. While still in its infancy, this area holds immense promise, and should be a major target area of the US Department of Education. Hybrid online / offline models for University *and* High School are, to me at least, the future. A country that spends close to a Trillion dollars a year on education would be well advised to make a significant investment in this area.

Where We Are: Not A Good Place.

One of our key thesis in Chapter 5, is that the fundamental currency of the future is information, intellectual capital. It is not as important for the United States to own or house the assembly lines that mass produce the next iPhone as it is to have the engineers, the designers, and the management to *create* the next iPhone. This means an educated workforce, and unfortunately, the United States is showing signs of lagging in this area.

Certainly at the very high end, the US still has the best universities (Stanford, Harvard, MIT etc..) and has produced the most Nobel Laureates[43] (349 for the US, 116 for the UK, 101 Germany, 66 France, 8 China, 7 India). But the overall number of college graduates per capita is now second tier.

For a country with some of the finest universities in the world, the US actually is quite behind the rest of the OECD when it comes to actually finishing college.

90%	Japan
80%	Germany
80%	France
80%	Australia
70%	UK
50%	USA

Percentage of Students Who Start University And Finish

And It is worse with regard to Scientists.

According to Fortune[44], China now Graduates 10,000 engineering PhDs per year versus 8,000 for the US. And for bachelors degrees in engineering, math, computer science and information technology, China claims 500,000 annual graduates versus 150,000 in the US. Even if overstated, these statistics are somewhat alarming; increasingly Chinese born US university graduates are choosing to go back home as opposed to staying in the US. The one key advantage the US still has over the rest of world – greater technology and innovation – could very well be ending.

As an employer and science PhD myself, I can attest to the severity of the problem from a recruiting perspective. Whether in the San Francisco Bay Area, Los Angeles or North Carolina, it is extremely difficult to find and retain qualified engineering talent. Companies like Google and Facebook have massive efforts aimed at importing Chinese and Indian talent in under H1-B work visas. Some companies have resorted to having engineers live and work on ships moored just outside of international water boundaries.

The problem starts at the K-12 level, and is primarily a state problem, not a federal one.

Education as a Percentage of GDP

Education is one of the single largest components of modern economies, significantly bigger than Defense. Its worth getting one's head around the numbers:

Sweden	7.0%
Finland	6.8%
UK	6.2%
France	5.9%
US	5.4%
Switzerland	5.2%
Germany	5.1%

Japan	3.8%
India	3.3%
Singapore	3.2%

Education As a Percentage of GDP. Source: World Bank 45

The pattern here is not surprising: the US and Europe are spending roughly the same overall percentages on education, with the heavily socialized Nordic countries (Sweden and Finland) leading the pack with 7%. Singapore is the most efficient, as usual, with just 3.2% spent on GDP – and I know from first hand experience that their education is excellent.

The number I want the reader to focus on here is 5%. That's ballpark what we are spending now on education as a percentage of our economy, and I believe that number should not go down. My core thesis is that we are moving from an industrial economy to a pure information economy. We need to invest in brainpower at all levels of our society, from kindergarten to the PhD level.

The Scope of our School System

The education of American children is the one of largest, most top-down systems man has ever undertaken. At any one time, about 54 million children are in Kindergarten through 12th Grade – twice the population of North Korea. Even broken down into 50 mainly independent state systems, that's a lot of people.

From an infrastructure point of view, the numbers are daunting:

- 13,588 School Districts
- 132,181 Schools
- 437,410 Teachers

In terms of kids, that's about 4 million for every grade, or a total of 17.6% of our entire population.

To put this in perspective, the largest franchise in the world, McDonalds operates 35,000 restaurants worldwide[46], and employs 1.7 million people. McDonalds and the US School System are similar in scope; McDonalds has one fourth as many locations, but employs four times as many people.

However, McDonalds, Hertz and other franchises only work by having a very narrow, standardized product offering. Schools are much more individual cases: hiring schoolteachers is more an art than a mass-market process; economic and cultural conditions for school districts vary greatly, and what we need to teach changes quickly.

Federal-Directed Curriculums Wont Work

At one point in the history of US Education, a simple curriculum of the three R's (Reading, Writing and Arithmetic) was direction enough. Not in today's quickly changing world.

Computer Science for example, was barely a field of study thirty years ago – today it is one of the most important. User Interface Design, Entrepreneurship and Biotechnology are some other emerging areas that didn't exist a generation ago.

The idea of having a national committee sit around a table and set forth a precise curriculum for K-12 is not optimal. A better approach is to let individual schools try a number of individual approaches, give parents the choice of where to send their children, and cut off funding for the ones that clearly are not working. This is the basic premise of Bush's No Child Left Behind (NCLB) and Bloomberg's reform projects in New York City.

As an aside, I (and millions of other student in France) suffered through the results of a different committee formed to decide how to teach mathematics in French high schools. This committee, influenced by the highly formal theoretical math group Bourbaki[47] decided that it was an excellent idea to teach 16 year olds group and commutative ring theory. While, I eventually discovered and learned to love this field of abstract algebra as a college sophomore majoring in Math, this approach made no sense at all for high school. Committees are notorious for coming to the worst consensuses.

Different People Want Different Things

Curriculum battles often are just one example where different people want perfectly reasonable, but different, things. To quote a Milton Friedman example[48] some people like green ties and other people like red ties. When you buy a product in the marketplace, you are "voting" for either green or red ties. Those voting for green ties will get green ties, while those voting for red ties will get red ties. On the other hand, if the government picks the color of the tie, we are all either getting red or green, irrespective of who in the government we voted for.

The Cato Institute has an interactive map[49] where you can visualize these battlegrounds geographically. Besides curriculum issues, these include:

Freedom of Expression. There is general disagreement over how much freedom students should have to "express themselves." For example, should "droopy pants" be allowed in schools? Alex Howard, Vice President of the Richmond County Board of Education did not think so. In support of the right, some students at Cross Creek High School held a "Pull your pants up!" rally[50]. Others disagreed. Eventually the school board won and droopy pants were banned.

Religion. Ronald Reagan famously campaigned for the right to prayer in school. More recently, many battles involve use of Christian words and phrases. For example, Poway Unified School District administrators ordered Brad Johnson, a math teacher at Westfield High School, to take down banners that had hung in his classroom for nearly two decades. "These are patriotic sayings that are inspiring to me," said Johnson. The banners included phrases such as "In God We Trust," and

"God Bless America". The case went all the way to the Supreme Court. Brad Johnson lost.

Reading Material. Not everybody agrees on what is and isn't appropriate reading material for kids. As an example, *In Our Mothers' House*, a book featuring a family with lesbian parents, was pulled from the shelves[51] of elementary schools in Davis School District. In another example, The *Adventures of Huckleberry Fin* offended black and Muslim leaders in Birdville Texas for using "The N Word." The superintendent wrote a letter of apology, and teachers received classes in cultural sensitivity.

Evolution. Although Europeans are generally of one mind when it comes to teaching the evolution of man, Americans are not. For example, The Alabama Board of Education voted unanimously to continue use of a disclaimer in biology textbooks stating that "evolution is a controversial theory[52]." Other boards have ruled differently. New Jersey Governor Chris Christie summed up the issue by saying he thinks it is "really a dangerous area for a governor who stands up from the top of the state to say, 'You should teach this, you shouldn't teach that." When asked whether he believes in creationism or evolution, Christie responded, "That's none of your business."

For all these issues there is no single right or wrong answer, and certainly no answer that can be decided by a single national or even state committee. As a believer in Science and Darwinism, it pains me that publicly funded schools teach something as blatantly wrong as creationism. But at the end of the day, if a creationist school can turn out seniors with high SAT scores, who am I to argue?

Historical Need For Conformity

In his book, Capitalism and Freedom[53] Friedman argues that the current state funded educational system might have once served a need for conformity. Indeed, with massive numbers of immigrants flooding the US in the late 19th century, it may well have been critical to set national standards for English and Math proficiency. Similar thoughts were behind the origins of the French Napoleonic "Baccalaureat" system.

Today, however, one size no longer fits all. We live in a world far beyond the "three R's." – even at the elementary school level. Different people truly have different needs; we need a much more flexible system than a state-designed curricula.

Bloomberg's Approach: Test, Prune

From 2001 to 2013, the billionaire Michael Bloomberg served as Mayor of New York City. One of his main areas of focus was public education; during those 12 years he continued the reforms initiated under George Bush, and took a quantitative approach to managing the nation's largest school system. Notes Diane Ravitch (a major *critic* of education reform)

"The Bloomberg administration's signature policy was closing schools and opening schools. Schools with low scores were closed and replaced. Large schools were closed and replaced. Some new schools were closed and replaced by other new schools."[54]

Bloomberg, like Bush, relied on standardized tests to determine which of the 1,700 public NY schools were running below acceptable standards. Like defective McDonalds franchises, those schools that did not meet the grade were closed, and in many cases replaced by private charter schools.

The results were disruptive, as change typically is. Teachers unions, and parents fearing change fought against the closures. Schools focused mainly on the narrow testing areas (reading and mathematics) disregarding subjects such as art. Critics like Ravitch longed for the "a balanced curriculum" ignoring the enormous problems that Bloomberg was solving.

In 2014, the new mayor of New York City, Bill De Blasio, started to unravel Bloomberg's legacy. Instead of supporting a tough, metrics driven approach to education, De Blasio is handing it back to the teachers unions, ending the expansion of charter schools and rewarding mediocrity in the NY school system.

Charter Schools

We've briefly mentioned charter schools, but its worth spending a bit more time on them. A charter school is by definition a private school that receives funding from the government. Because of our federal system, this (unfortunately) has to be state government, not national government.

The idea of charter schools dates only back to 1992. It's a growing concept. Today there are 5,600 charter schools educating about 2 million students nationwide[55] – about 4% of the overall educational system.

Because charter schools are typically run as for profit enterprises, they tend to be better run than unionized state run schools. On objective, standardized tests, charter schools come out ahead. And because they are not limited to narrowly defined school districts, they create an upgrade path for minorities looking to escape ghettos.

But, they are businesses, and as businesses they hire and fire employees, and sometimes fail, leaving parents who rely on them in the lurch. This is no different from any other aspect of the free-market economy. Your accounting software can also go out of business and fire the programmers who built it. That doesn't mean the government should write accounting software.

Accrediting charter schools, or anything else that gets government funding, should rely on continuous testing to make sure the government is getting its money's worth. The tests do not have to be as narrow as Bloomberg's NYC reading and mathematics tests. But schools should be objectively measured in a standardized way, and bad charter schools, as well as bad public schools should be eventually shut down.

These tests don't have to be black or white. It is very possible that a charter school could have only a *portion* of its costs covered by the state as opposed to the entirety. This mirrors the upgrade path to more expensive healthcare coverage. Right now, if you send your child to a private school you are in effect paying twice, once for the education you are using, and once for the free education you are not using. Partial coverage of a privately operated charter schools solves this problem (another option is by providing a tax benefit[56], but this complicates unnecessarily the idea of a flat tax).

It should be pointed out that the growth of charter schools is drawing students out of private schools[57] and hence adds to the overall *public share* of the education cost (but not to the cost of education overall).

Today, charter schools are being viewed as an alternative mainly when public schools clearly fail. But, I predict that privatization and choice will ultimately prevail, and charter schools will someday represent the *majority* of all schools. And many of them will be purely online.

Online Education

One of the most promising areas of all is online education. Khan Academy[58], an effort of a single person to put a number of simple courses online has proven beyond a shadow of a doubt that massive benefits can accrue from just a small investment in online courseware. This is *exactly* the kind of work that should be funded by grants from the federal government.

Coursera[59], is "an education platform that partners with top universities and organizations worldwide, to offer courses online for anyone to take, for free." Only a few years old, and the content on the site is starting to be excellent. I took the Coursera graduate level course on quantum mechanics and enjoyed it immensely.

As the Cato Institute notes[60], online education blurs state boundaries, and even national boundaries. There is no reason that students shouldn't be able to take foreign online courses if they are cost efficient.

> "The growth of online education will make international trade in higher education services far more common. And in response to this increasing trade, there are likely to be complaints about the impact of foreign competition on domestic institutions."

Down the road, it is conceivable that the US government could re-reimburse these foreign online education vendors. The "Buy American Act[61]" passed in 1933 requires the US government to prefer US made products and services, but it doesn't completely exclude foreign ones. With vast numbers of cheap, educated tutors, hybrid models featuring online courses with long-distance human grading and tutoring could become an extremely viable alternative to classrooms.

Micklethwait argues[62] that the idea that you need millions of schoolteachers to adequately deliver a quality educational service may not be as absolute as we think. Just as technology has made agriculture and manufacturing dramatically more efficient, it can, and is, being used to automate and improve the delivery of services. Baumol's law is being repealed.

Incentivizing Students

Besides providing completely funded and partially funded choices for parents, including online options, the government should consider incentivizing students directly. Like fitness, gamification principles apply – by offering national recognition and cash incentives for achieving certain educational milestones (such as proficiency in a foreign language, leaning computer programing skills, or passing an advanced mathematics test) could be very motivating.

These "badges" could be available for students to display prominently on their online web identities (their websites, resume sites on programs such as LinkedIn, or on their social media pages). They would click through to a verifiable government page indicating that Fred Krueger of Santa Monica CA, for example, is fluent in English and French, has an advanced knowledge of statistics and computer programming, and is a qualified tutor. Standardization of these pages would have significant advantages for recruiting, and, in my opinion would in and of itself push students to achieve more.

Adding a small cash component could make the incentive even more appealing. In my field of mathematics, for example, the Hungarian mathematician Paul Erdos[63] used to give out small monetary prizes for researchers who could help him solve mathematical problems. This is brilliantly documented in the movie N is a Number[64]; "Paul Erdos liked to ask new questions, and quite often offers money for their solutions" notes Laszlo Lovasz, a professor of combinatorics. Eventually these monetary awards became badges of honor in the mathematical field.

Education – Summary.

Education is an enormous part of our economy – about 5%. It is not a place we should look to save money on, but change is needed on *how* we spend that money. The long term solution is to have privately organized schools compete for parent's votes and dollars. Exactly as with healthcare, a basic level of education, whether it is provided for by public or private schools should be available to everybody, but parents should have the option to choose a type of school that makes sense for them. The only caveat is that federally or state funded institutions should be vetted and continuously reviewed to make sure they are providing good value for government money.

Like Healthcare, the current poor state of affairs is a golden opportunity for entrepreneurs and investors. Some of the same themes apply: taking the process online, using foreign workers as well as domestic ones, using cash incentives and badges to "gamify the system"

12. Protecting the Environment

THE ENVIRONMENT IS NOT A MAJOR LINE ITEM OF THE US BUDGET, but its ultimately one the single most important factors in our overall quality of life. We only have one planet, and despite dreams of some of my fellow technologists to colonize Mars, there is really nowhere else to live within a trillion miles. On a much more mundane level, ask any New Yorker how they would feel if we turned Central Park into a new real estate development. It might solve NY City's budget problems for a few years, but it would subtract so much from the average person's experience of the city.

Having said this, like Defense, protecting the environment comes at a cost. There are good and bad ways of going about it. Large committees and energy departments are not the answer, nor are a lot of red tape around every conceivable commercial operation. The key is to incentivize a low level of pollution and carbon emissions, by taxing these "externalities" at the correct level. And the correct level is to tolerate some abuse – it will happen anyways – but heavily discourage significant destruction of our environmental heritage.

It's also important to really look at the facts. Is bio-diesel really a benefit to the environment, even though supported by Willie Nelson and a large percentage of corn farmers in Iowa? Are high speed trains and electric cars really the answer just because they appear "clean"? The number one source of "clean electricity" right now is "dirty coal", which is far and away the major source of global warming. Solar energy certainly seems promising, but what is the best way to incentivize that? Funding startups like Solyndra[65] has proven to be a horrible idea. We need better solutions.

Fortunately, others, including the Cato Institute, have thought long and hard about this issue. We will quote them heavily here, as we are heavily aligned on the subject.

Environmental Regulation

As Milton Friedman argued in Free To Choose[66],

> "Public discussion of the environmental issue is frequently characterized by more emotion than reason. Much of it proceeds as if the issue was pollution versus no pollution, as if it were desirable or possible to have a world without pollution. This is clearly nonsense... We could have a world without pollution from automobiles by simply abolishing all automobiles... but the cost would clearly exceed the gain."

The key, then is putting a price tag on the negative "externalities" created by pollution, global warming, and other negative environmental effects, and charging those responsible, incrementally in direct proportion to the damage they create. Again, the focus is on (dis)incentives, not laws. Let individuals and companies make their own choices, but make them pay if they harm the common welfare.

The hard-core environmental movement as represented by activists like Greenpeace [67] and the National Resource Defense Council[68] are actually doing the environmental cause a huge disservice by overstating risks, dramatizing events, and making everything a black and white issue. The Cato Institute takes a much more thoughtful, reasoned approach:

> "Science can inform individual preferences but cannot resolve environmental conflicts. Environmental goods and services, to the greatest extent possible, should be treated like other goods and services in the marketplace. People should be free to secure their preferences about the consumption of environmental goods such as clean air or clean water regardless of whether some scientists think such preferences are legitimate or not. Likewise, people should be free, to the greatest extent possible, to make decisions consistent with their own risk tolerances regardless of scientific or even public opinion."

Global Warming

The scientific evidence for global warming is straightforward. If any reader has doubts, I would refer him or her to the website of Intergovernmental Panel on Climate Change[69] (IPCC), and the massive studies undertaken by that organization, comprised of the world's leading scientists.

But while it is a scientific fact that the planet is getting, slowly, a very little bit warmer every year, it is also very easy to exaggerate and dramatize the risks as Al Gore did[70] in his move "An Inconvenient Truth."

Its also a very, very difficult issue to solve. For the US to take unilateral action, and for example, tax carbon emissions will not solve the problem *globally*, as long as China builds a new coal plant every week. And this is, truly, a global issue. There are no shortcuts; or as the Cato Institute concludes:

> "Global warming is indeed real, and human activity has been a contributor since 1975. But global warming is also a very complicated and difficult issue that can provoke very unwise policy in response to political pressure."

Natural Resources

The use of our natural resources – in particular energy resources – has been a lightning rod for both parties. The left have taken a draconian view that all ecological resources are "by definition public property, or commons, that must be centrally planned and stewarded by bureaucratic agents lest they be recklessly despoiled by industry."[71] The right on the other hand, have insinuated that by opening up Alaska and other areas for drilling we will return to $2 Gas and energy independence. Sarah Palin's "Drill, Baby, Drill" mantra typifies this position.

The truth is somewhere in the middle. We should look carefully at the costs and benefits of further exploiting our resources, and balance these with all the other aspects of government, many of which go in opposite directions. To quote the Cato Institute[72] again:

> "It makes no sense for the federal government to subsidize environmental destruction on one hand while establishing laws, regulations, and vast bureaucracies to mitigate it on the other. Reconsidering those subsidies would help not only the environment but the economy as well."

Energy

Ronald Reagan famously campaigned to eliminate the department of Energy[73] created by Jimmy Carter in 1977. Today, this $28 Billion monstrosity spends half of its money looking after the nations nuclear arsenal (hiding some of our bloated defense costs in this very un-defense sounding department), and the other half in dreaming up counter-productive plans to achieve "energy independence".

The track record of the DOE is abysmal. As the Cato Institute concludes:

> "Energy, like other goods and services in the economy, should be left to consumers and entrepreneurs in the market, not "planned" by governmental bodies. In fact, the long history of U.S. oil, gas, and electricity regulation, taxation, and subsidization makes abundantly clear that shortages and energy crises are engendered by government intervention, not market failure."

The Environment – Summary.

Our position on the environment is squarely in the middle of modern political debate. We acknowledge the long term risks of global warming and the overall importance of preserving a clean, sustainable environment, but we caution against too much regulation and quick conclusions. This is more of an area which deserves a careful eye as opposed to being the center-piece for political reform.

13. A Plan of Action

Where We Stand

"The road to hell", as the saying goes, "Is paved with good intentions." Under the guise of a lot of perfectly reasonable ideas ("provide decent jobs to decent Americans", "protect America and respect the men and woman who serve our country", "give poor folks a chance" etc..), the system that is the federal and state government has evolved into a barely functional, autonomous organism that is on the verge of choking our entire economy.

The problem is not so much a US one as general problem with democracies at this stage in history. With very few exceptions, all modern economies are in the same boat that we are in, with massive government bureaucracies, debt to GDP ratios that are mathematically untenable, tax laws that are so complex that nobody understands them, and rampant fraud and abuse at every stage of the system.

The "software" that forms the basis of our political system is old, complex and buggy – like a piece of 1980 IBM Cobol code. It can't be fixed by incremental changes, or "patches"; it needs to be re-written. You can't create an iPhone out of old Motorola software; nor can you take a typical DMV and turn it into an Apple Store. You need to start over.

Prioritizing Change

Radical changes cannot be made without significant pain and disruption. You don't go from royalty to democracy without casualties – and not only at the top. But this doesn't mean that all the changes described here need to be made at once. Just like in software re-design, it's best to start with one or two of the most important problems, and work your way down from the top to the least critical ones. This is how I see one possible progression:

1. Election of a president with a strong libertarian bias. This could be a Reagan style republican, A third party candidate, or conceivably (but not likely) a new mold of democrat.

2. Passing a flat tax and a balanced budget amendment. This will clean up the revenue side of the balance sheet, and get us to our first balanced budget in decades. It will also mean enormous pain for military contractors, the healthcare industry, retirees. It will be messy, but we will live.

3. Healthcare reform, with a simplified, national plan, incentives for choice and competition and passing a patients right to data bill.

4. Welfare reform. Once we have a flat tax, balanced budget and national heath care, the foundations will be in place for a complete simplification of all other entitlements.

5. The elimination of social security and inclusion of it within the overall flat tax / flat benefits approach. This will dramatically simplify the government's accounting

6. The Elimination of agricultural subsidies, all foreign tariffs, and a simplification and easing of immigration policies. By this point, the economic benefits of the overall plan should be clear to all.

7. Educational reform, with a voucher based system, focus on choice and competition, and, like for healthcare reform, a national focus, as opposed to state-by-state.

Throughout this process, we should endeavor to bring our overall software infrastructure up to 21rst century standards. We should have a universal login, pay our taxes and vote online. This is not so much a "checkbox" as it is an ongoing commitment to "clean up our code."

The Political Landscape

The political story of 2010 was the rise of the tea party. But while the tea party has been derided for its right wing social platforms, anti-immigration bent and nationalism, a strong undercurrent of libertarianism percolated through it[74]. As Charles Krauthammer noted in the Washington Post: "Libertarianism has gone from the fringes to a position of prominence in a major party." More than any other person, Ron Paul has channeled this new responsible, acceptable libertarian doctrine. I subscribe to much of it.

Technologists such as Peter Thiel, economic writers such as Mickelthwait and Wooldridge, and think tanks such as the Cato Institute and are adding a new, clear, outside the beltway perspective to the debate. Just as industrialists supported the free-trade and free-market principles that drove the massive progress of the 19th and 20th centuries, the "digerati" may very well be the ones to lead us into a new, rationalized form of 21st century government.

Conclusions.

The United States has some clear advantages over any other country in the world. We are blessed with lots of land, vast natural resources (in particular, vast energy resources), and a human population that, at least historically, has had one of the most "can do", opportunistic attitudes of any culture. Our legal system protects intellectual property, allows simple company formation, hiring and firing, and while not perfect, is far more business friendly than most nations.

Our main problem now is our government "software." Will we, as a nation, have the courage and the vision to throw out the old and start with something clean and new? We have mobilized before – in 1776, at the formation of the nation, and in 1941, when we joined World War II. But, as in those decision points, success is not guaranteed. It is entirely possible that the US fails, and joins Babylon, ancient Rome, the Ottoman Empire and countless other failed civilizations on the junk heap of History.

What I and others are proposing is hard, maybe even impossible. But as Victor Hugo said the night before he died: "One resists the invasion of armies; one does not resist the invasion of ideas.[75]" The ideas here are offered to anyone who can use them. I am cautiously optimistic.

Fred Krueger

Further Reading

This book was a big undertaking (and still is, as I am sure I will be revising and editing it for quite a long time). In this section I wanted to go over some of my sources and give the reader additional areas to expand his or her personal understanding of the subject.

The year being 2014, many of these sources are websites with long URLs, online videos or PDFs that can be downloaded online. Others are physical books that can bought on Amazon, or downloaded on various devices. In general, I will try to give the reader enough information to find it using Google or another search engine, as opposed to a domain or an ISBN number.

I will also be keeping a purely online version of this book in interactive format at www.simplify.club (note the new top level domain extension). This version was created in my own web publishing tool, Mozart. You can comment on all or part of it at this address, or reach me online. I look forward to hearing from you.

Economics and Economic History

Free To Choose, by Milton Friedman is a book published in 1980 that followed a 10 part PBS Series on Free Market Capitalism that can be viewed in its entirety on YouTube. The book and the TV series both ended up being best sellers; I highly recommend both.

Capitalism and Freedom, by Milton Friedman, is a book originally published in 1962 which discusses the role of economic capitalism in a liberal society.

The Rise and Decline of Nations, by Mancur Olson (1982) is, in my opinion a seminal study on how collective bargaining over time will dramatically lower growth. Olson is an economist, and the book too often feels like an economics textbook, but the analysis is profound.

The Road To Serfdom, is a book by the Austrian Economist Friederich Von Hayak written in 1943, which argues that classic liberalism results in the loss of freedom. It's a bit of rant, somewhat dated, and not the easiest read, but there are gems of wisdom there that you will find nowhere else.

The Flat Tax, by Hall and Rabushka, is a book published in 2007 that goes over the fully developed flat tax theories of these two Hover Institution economists.

The Fourth Revolution, by Mickelthwait and Wooldridge, is a 2014 analysis of the failures of the welfare state by two contributors to The Economist. It is beyond brilliant – going into the historical formation of the modern nation state, and the evolution of it into the choking mass of complexity and special interests we now find ourselves in.

Republic Lost, How Money Corrupts Congress and a Plan To Stop It, by Larry Lessig (2012) is a compelling story, meticulously researched, that Congress has now reached a stage of full corruption. His solution is widespread mobilization and a new constitution.

The Big Short, Inside the Doomsday Machine, by Michael Lewis, is a brilliantly written analysis of both our 2008 subprime loan problem and Europe's equivalent subprime country problem, with Iceland, Greece and Ireland each being brilliantly dissected.

Griftopia: Bubble Machines, Vampire Squids, and the Long Con That Is Breaking America, by Matt Taibbi in 2010, is an excellent account of the 2009 Financial Crisis, written from a leftist point of view. My biggest takeaway from this book was the degree that Goldman Sachs (and other banks) had infiltrated Washington up to, during, and immediately after the crisis.

Running on Empty written in 2005 by Pete Peterson (the billionaire founder of Blackrock), was an early warning of the budget predicament that we now find ourselves in. A bit alarming, and not to be taken completely to the letter, but interesting nevertheless.

Technology

The Innovator's Dilemma, by Clay Christenson of Harvard University is mentioned in our chapter on healthcare and is an excellent and seminal work on how technological change occurs – not by creating better products, but by creating cheaper products that are *good enough*.

Health Care

Where Does it Hurt, by Jonathan Bush was recently released (May 2014) and is – in my opinion – an excellent overview of what exactly is wrong with the current American healthcare system. The author, a nephew of the 43rd president, has true entrepreneurial chops – having founded Athena Health[76], a 2Billion dollar leader in medical billing and records.

Education

The Death and Life of the Great American School System, by Diane Ravitch (2010) is a critical analysis of educational reform. It's a useful book to read to understand how anti-reformers think; it's well researched, written from the heart, and comes to exactly the wrong conclusions.

Energy and the Environment

Energy For Future Presidents, by Richard Muller (2012), is an account of Climate Change and Energy Alternatives, from the viewpoint of a skeptical, but extremely well informed scientist. Muller (who I have met several times) knows global warming better than anyone. His views on Fukashima and the BP Oil Spill will shock you.

Think Tanks

The Cato Institute (www.cato.org) is a libertarian think tank headquartered in Washington DC and founded in 1974. Despite being funded by the somewhat notorious Koch brothers, the institute produces, in my opinion some of the very best research out there. The research direction is libertarian – not republican. In particular, the institute has come down strongly against George Bush (as well as Obama).

The Heritage Foundation (www.heritage.org) is a conservative think tank, also based in Washington DC. The foundation produces many excellent data pieces, sometimes in conjunction with the Wall Street Journal, but in my opinion is too closely allied with mainstream Republican dogma, in particular in its prior support for Operation Desert Storm. Still, a good source of data.

Timbro (http://timbro.se/en) is a Swedish think tank who's mission is to originate, promote and disseminate ideas and issues supporting the principles of free markets, free enterprise, individual liberty and a free society. It publishes a number of highly-rated economic studies in book format.

Reform (http://www.reform.co.uk/) is a British think tank focused primarily on health care with ties to the Tony Blair government.

General Books on Simplicity

The Laws of Simplicity, by John Maeda, is a short, entertaining analysis of how simplicity works in modern design. Maeda is a professor of design at the MIT Media Lab, and echoes many of my thoughts on simplicity / complexity from the Introduction. Maeda break down the different components of simplicity (removing features, hiding features etc..) that affect the design process.

Rework, by Jason Fried and David Heinemeier Hanson (cofounders of the Internet Service Basecamp) is a re-think of what work should look like in the 21rst century. Fried and Hanson should know – they have built an awesome product in a very unconventional way, using a mainly distributed workforce.

End Notes

The Process

At 53, I would have never picked myself as the kind of person likely to write a book, let alone two. But a painful divorce, followed by a complete personal transformation forced "Stop Drinking and Get Fit!77" from me; and after writing one book, it's extremely tempting to try it again.

Many people ask me how long it takes, and how I did it; so here is my technique:

First of all, I start with Microsoft Word and define a number of key styles for chapter titles, headings paragraph text and pull quotes. For this book, I chose Garamond, a classic Serif font as my base style. Garamond was first used in 1530, and still to this day is one of the most beautiful creations in the history of typography. Fonts really matter: Garamond felt appropriate for the subject matter, but it would completely out of place for other types of books. I would urge you to find out more about fonts and typography if you are at all interested in writing.

I should emphasize and re-emphasize the need to use names, defined custom styles. One of the classic beginners mistakes is to manually style things like headings or chapter titles, instead of defining and using a named style. This makes it much more difficult to try different styles globally, and to do things like create a table of contents.

Once I had the basic formatting in place I worked on the book primarily at night and weekends. My Goal was to produce a book of roughly 40,000 words – twice the size of my previous book. For me, this word count was to become my key progress indicator.

To see how this works, take any book you want to duplicate, and select a few pages at random. A good example is a book quoted here several times, "Where Does it Hurt" by Jonathan Bush. If you look at that book, you will see the following pattern

200 pages
Roughly 28 lines per page
Roughly 12 words per line

Multiplying these out you get 28 * 12 = 330 words per page and 67,000 = 28 * 12 * 200 words in total. This is about average. I personally prefer a significantly less dense style with about 200 words per page (extra line between paragraphs, 20 lines per page, 10 words per line) – but there is no "right answer".

In a single sitting I find that I can write between 600 and 1,400 words – or between 3 and 7 pages. Using the average of 1,000 words you can then see it takes about 50 sittings to finish a book this size. Working on it 3 days a week translates into 16 weeks – 4 months.

Once you have your basic word count, then the real difficulty begins. An editor is a necessity; I found one easily on craigslist (Marza Panzer), and at a fairly low cost was able to get her to correct the innumerable spelling and grammar mistakes that Microsoft Word did not pick up. It's a painful process; at the beginning you are excited to have produced an actual book, but by the fiftieth time you re-read it, it no longer seems at all interesting or even worthwhile. But with a month or so of editing, you at this point have a decent first draft.

Now is the time to turn what you have into an actual book. There are several ways to do this, but the simplest is to use the service from Amazon called "Create Space[78]". This service is pure publishing on demand. You simply upload your book (and pick a cover, which you will typically need a graphic designer and / or a photographer to help you with) and Amazon will print out copies on demand. You can set the price you charge, and you automatically get a revenue share off the top. It's a great system.

Like Software As A Service, where you can modify your software at any time, Publishing On Demand allows you to easily upload new editions of your book as you make revisions. This is an amazing thing, as you will in fact want to revise your book often, well beyond the point where you are fact completely sick of it.

I found that it was handy to give people actual printed copies of my book to write as opposed to electronic copies (PDFs) or copies printed from my office printer and bound together at the local copy shop. The minute people see an actual book they take it much more seriously, and the comments that you get are of a much higher quality.

People

I would like to thank the following people for reading and commenting on various drafts of this book:

Jim Willenborg, many of whose ideas I agree with, and a few I do not: notably the need for an oversized defense.

Antony Van Couvering, my business partner, who falls much more to the left of the political spectrum than me, but nevertheless read it with an open min.

Robert Krueger, my father, who was particularly helpful on the economic and banking sections.

Julian Rose, a former colleague of mine at Salomon Brothers, and one of smartest minds I have met in the Financial Markets.

Notes

1   The length of the tax code keeps growing: http://goo.gl/Af7TXd

2   At the time of this writing Amazon Fresh is only available in Seattle and Los Angeles: fresh.amazon.com

3   Gorbachev on Parkinson: http://goo.gl/Fr0iLf

4   This Lyndon Johnson quote is from "The Fourth Revolution". The original source is here: http://goo.gl/1k3

5   Bernard Baruch has some excellent quotes: http://goo.gl/aoMt8

6   The Rise and Decline of Nations, Mancur Olson 1982.

7   Baumol's Cost Disease has a decent Wikipedia page: http://goo.gl/twQdY

8   Quantcast is an accurate source of site traffic: http://goo.gl/7rgFzX

9   The Wealth of Nations is a very long, but extremely readable book: http://goo.gl/9TtL2h

---

10   "Irrational Exuberance" by Robert Schiller:
http://www.irrationalexuberance.com/

11   Daniel Kahneman, "Thinking Fast and Slow"
http://goo.gl/fjm93Z

12   Free To Choose: http://goo.gl/YEY0e

13   The history of Nucor is remarkable.
http://www.nucor.com/story

14   Charlie Rose interviews Lee Kwan Yu: http://goo.gl/Tk0jzW

15   See The Fourth Revolution, Micklethwait and Wooldridge, Chapter 3, "Beatrice Webb and the Welfare State".

16   Beatrice   Web   was   the   godmother   of   socialism
http://en.wikipedia.org/wiki/Beatrice_Webb

17   The   Japan   that   can   say   no   was   a   1980's   classic:
http://goo.gl/sdgUky

18   The Japanese "Recruit Scandal": http://goo.gl/uodwQI

19   Rambus is a 1.5 Billion Market Cap company, with no operations. http://www.rambus.com/

20   T   he Cato Institute has a great discussion on why the mortgage deduction should be eliminated. http://goo.gl/sa5U2j

21   Steven Teles "Kludgeocracy in America": http://goo.gl/U0Y0S3

22   This is from the Heritage Foundation: http://goo.gl/iqMhoN

23   How   To   Spend   3.9   Trillion   (Cato   Institute):
http://goo.gl/BaPwhw

24   Where does it Hurt? is a great analysis of what ails healthcare. http://goo.gl/zfnWRw

25   Epic   is   Enterprise   Software   for   Healthcare. http://www.epic.com/

26   Center For Disease Control Study

27   Fat taxes have been discussed at length, but are politically difficult. Positive incentives are a better idea. http://goo.gl/UgBi

28   FitBit (www.fitbit.com) is leading the way in wearable devices.

29   Nike Fuel band. http://goo.gl/1ydR70

30   Low Cost Heart Surgery In India: http://goo.gl/zwKpjI

31   St Goran's hospital in Sweden: http://goo.gl/o7BXKf

32   The Obama "Death Squads": http://goo.gl/l9Uf1D

33   The Heritage Foundation is an authority on welfare / entitlement data. http://goo.gl/rM6KuZ

34   Disability USA is a must watch 60 minutes episode (available on YouTube). http://goo.gl/vg1hKB

35   The home of the disability insurance fund on the Governments' social security "portal" http://www.ssa.gov/disability/

36   Binder and Binder is a leading disability law firm, featured in 60 Minutes'   blistering   attack   on   Disability   scams: http://www.binderandbinder.com/

37   The Cato Institute argues in favor of relaxed immigration: http://goo.gl/WjFjNu

38   The Cost of the Iraq War keeps going up: http://goo.gl/Gg2piI

39   Not all Republicans are in favor of runaway defense spending: http://goo.gl/mtIwGK

---

40   The rising cost of veteran disability: http://goo.gl/tnmZPH

41   Free to Choose was a 10 part PBS series, now viewable on YouTube: http://goo.gl/TsZddK

42   Lynn Cheney's attack on the teaching of history: http://hnn.us/article/8418

43   Nobel Laureates, by Country. http://goo.gl/hiidi

44   China's PHD Crop: http://goo.gl/rbTrd

45   Public spending on education, total (% of GDP): http://goo.gl/h3I5f

46   Source: McDonald's website: http://goo.gl/eZSMp

47   99% of French Science Majors have no idea they owe their deficient math education to Bourbaki. http://goo.gl/PKoNFW

48   Milton Friedman, Free to Choose. http://goo.gl/YEY0e

49   Cato has an interactive map showing local issues in education. Worth checking out. http://www.cato.org/education-fight-map

50   Droopy Pants controversy: http://goo.gl/6bAzNq

51   Banned Books: "In our mother's house." http://goo.gl/LgSjWb

52   In Alabama, Evolution is "a controversial theory": http://goo.gl/5R5nqA

53   Capitalism And Freedom, Chapter 6. http://goo.gl/7t0XpI

54   Bloomberg's educational reforms are being unraveled as we speak. http://goo.gl/0SD0v3

55   Stats on Charter Schools: http://goo.gl/nkUC9x

56   "Donating The Tax Voucher An Alternative Tax Treatment of Private School Enrollment" Cato Institute. http://goo.gl/TjaDsH

57   The impact of charter schools on private school enrollment: http://goo.gl/RXjF4w

58   The Khan Academy is an impressive achievement, originally of a single human being. https://www.khanacademy.org/

59   Coursera is a private company that is innovating heavily in the education space. www.coursera.org. (also see: http://goo.gl/v0ffwd)

60   Cross Border Education: http://goo.gl/T0cpNA

61   The "Buy American Act" http://goo.gl/9cMucq

62   The Fourth Revolution – Baumol's Law and Education.

63   Paul Erdos. http://goo.gl/L30SVX

64   http://goo.gl/ZErxTFThe use of money as an incentive is discussed at 22min.

65   Solyndra, Obama's solar embarrassment: http://goo.gl/4q9zId

66   Free to Choose on Pollution: http://goo.gl/g116sy

67   Greenpeace criticism: http://goo.gl/MgfmHn

68   NRDC critique: http://goo.gl/BTPKVF

69   The home of the Intergovernmental Panel on Climate Change. http://www.ipcc.ch/

70   See in particular Richard Muller's criticism http://goo.gl/wUQoHi

71   Cato on the left environmental

72   Cato on Natural Resources. http://goo.gl/AuJ0vc

73   The Department of Energy: http://goo.gl/Awvsa

74   The Libertarian Roots of The Tea Party: http://goo.gl/RtAULD

75   Victor Hugo's Great Quote on Ideas: http://goo.gl/vBIC

76   Athena Health: http://goo.gl/KqUsDn

77   My own book on Drinking and Fitness: http://goo.gl/E6shCe

78   Amazon's self publishing platform: www.createspace.com